ROBERT GRAVES

MODERN LITERATURE MONOGRAPHS

GENERAL EDITOR: Lina Mainiero

In the same series:

(Continued on last page of book)

ROBERT GRAVES

Katherine Snipes

FREDERICK UNGAR PUBLISHING CO.
NEW YORK

Copyright © 1979 by Frederick Ungar Publishing Co., Inc.
Printed in the United States of America
Design by Anita Duncan

Library of Congress Cataloging in Publication Data

Snipes, Katherine, 1922–
    Robert Graves.

    Bibliography: p.
    Includes index.
    1. Graves, Robert, 1895–   —Criticism and inter-
pretation.   2.   Graves, Robert, 1895–   —Knowledge—
Folklore, mythology.   3.   Mythology in literature.
PR6013.R35Z79   821'.9'12   78-20943
ISBN 0-8044-2825-5

Contents

Chronology

July 24, 1895   Born at Wimbledon, England, to Alfred Percival Graves and Amalie von Ranke Graves.

1914   World War I declared. Graves joins the Royal Welsh Fusiliers.

1915   Graves is sent to the western front in France.

1916   Publishes first book of poetry, *Over the Brazier*. Meets Siegfried Sassoon at the front, a friendship to last many years.

July 20, 1916   Seriously wounded in France, listed as dead.

1917   Returns to front, but is immobilized by bronchitis. Graves is sent to Somerville College at Oxford, which has been converted into a hospital. Publishes *Fairies and Fusiliers*, poetry.

Sassoon is wounded in the neck and returned to England. Sassoon publishes a denunciation of the war. To prevent his friend from being courtmartialed, Graves gets a medical board to agree that Sassoon needs psychiatric care. Graves and Sassoon meet Dr. W. H. R. Rivers, whose theories about the creative imagination influenced Graves for several years.

January, 1918   Marries Nancy Nicholson, painter, socialist, feminist. In February, Graves is transferred to Rhyl where Nancy can join him.

1919   Graves is demobilized from the military. He and Nancy rent a cottage on John Masefield's estate. First child, Jenny, is born. Publishes *Treasure Box*, poetry.

1920   Publishes *Country Sentiment*, poetry. Second child, a son, is born.

1921   Robert and Nancy fail at an attempt at being shopkeepers. T. E. Lawrence gives Graves four chapters of *Seven Pillars of Wisdom* to sell for serial publication in the United States. The family moves to Islip. Publishes *The Pier-glass*, poetry.

1922   Publishes his first book of criticism, *On English Poetry*. Second girl child, Catherine, is born.

1923   Publishes *The Feather Bed* and *Whipperginny*, both poetry.

1924   Publishes *Mock Beggar Hall*, poetry. He is awarded the Bronze Medal for Poetry, Olympic Games, Paris. A second son, Sam, is born.

1925   Publishes *The Marmosite's Miscellany* and *Welshman's Hose*, poetry; *Poetic Unreason and Other Studies*, criticism; and *My Head! My Head!*, first historical novel.

1926   Gets his Bachelor of Letters, St. John's College, Oxford. Goes to Egypt with the family and new friend, Laura Riding, to become lecturer at Cairo University. Publishes *Another Future of Poetry* and *Impenetrability; or the Proper Habit of English*.

1927   Resigns his position in Cairo and returns to London. Publishes *Lawrence and the Arabs*, biography; *A Survey of Modernist Poetry*, with Laura Riding; *Poems 1914–1926*; *Poems 1914–1927*.

1928   Graves and Riding start Seizin Press in London.

1929   Domestic crisis—Nancy leaves—Graves allies himself with Laura Riding after she injures herself seriously by jumping from a fourth-story window. Graves writes his autobiography, *Good-Bye to All That*, also the short story "The Shout." Graves and Riding settle in Déya, Majorca, reestablish Seizin Press, publish critical magazine *Epilogue*.

1932   Collaborates with Riding on satirical novel *No Decency Left*.

1933   Publishes *The Real David Copperfield*.

1934   Publishes the Claudius novels.

1935   Receives Hawthornden Prize, oldest of the famous British literary prizes, for *I, Claudius*.

Receives James Tait Black Memorial Prize, administered through University of Edinburgh for the year's best novel, for *I, Claudius* and *Claudius the God*.

1936   Spanish Civil War forces evacuation from Majorca on twenty-four hours notice.

1938   Publishes *Count Belisarius*.

1939   Femina Vie Heureuse—Srock Prize.

Graves and Riding come to America—stay in a farmhouse owned by Schuyler Jackson, American poet. Other members of the living group: David Reeves, Alan and Beryl Hodge, Tom and Julie Matthews, Schuyler and Kit Jackson. Schuyler divorces his wife, marries Laura Riding; Graves returns to England.

Beryl Hodge divorces Alan and marries Graves in England.

1940   Collaborates with Alan Hodge in writing *The Long Week-End. A Social History of Great Britain 1918–1939*. Writes *Sergeant Lamb of the Ninth* (in United States, published as *Roger Lamb's America*).

1941   Publishes sequel, *Proceed, Sergeant Lamb*.

1943   Publishes *The Story of Marie Powell, Wife to Mr. Milton* and (with Alan Hodge) *Reader over Your Shoulder*.

1944   Publishes *The Golden Fleece* (in United States, published as *Hercules, My Shipmate*)

1945   Publishes *The White Goddess*.

1946   Returns to Majorca with Beryl and their three children, William, Lucia, and Juan. (A fourth child, Tomas, named after T. S. Matthews, is born later in Majorca.) Publishes *King Jesus*.

1949   Publishes *The Common Asphodel—Collected Essays on Poetry, Seven Days in New Crete* (*Watch the North Wind Rise*, in the United States), *The Islands of Unwisdom* (*The Isles of Unwisdom*, in the United States).

1950   Publishes *Occupation: Writer*, translates Lucius Apuleius's *The Transformations of Lucius*.

1953   Publishes *The Nazarene Gospel Restored*, in collaboration with Joshua Podro.

1954   Clark lecturer, Trinity College, Cambridge.

1955   Translates Manuel de Jesus Galvan's *The Cross and the Sword* and Pedro Antonio de Alarcon's *The Infant with the Globe*.
        Publishes *Homer's Daughter*; the two-volume reference work, *The Greek Myths*; *The Crowning Privilege*, criticism; *Collected Poems*.

1957   Publishes *They Hanged My Saintly Billy*; translates Gaius Suetonius Granquillus's *The Twelve Caesars*.

1958   Loines Award for Poetry, established by the friends of Russell Loines, who presented the fund to the National Institute of Arts and Letters. Publishes *5 Pens in Hand*.

1959   *Collected Poems* published; translates Homer's Iliad—*The Anger of Achilles*.

1960   William Foyle Poetry Prize for the *Collected Poems* as the most outstanding volume of verse published in the United Kingdom.

1961   M. A., Oxford University.
        Collected Poems, More Poems published.

1961–1966   Professor of Poetry at Oxford University.

1962   Arts Council Poetry Award; publishes *Oxford Addresses on Poetry*.

1963   Arthur Dehon Little Memorial Lecturer, Massachusetts Institute of Technology, Cambridge. Publishes *Nine Hundred Iron Chariots*.

1964   Publishes *The Hebrew Myths: The Book of Genesis* in collaboration with Raphael Patai; *Man Does, Woman Is* (poetry); *Collected Short Stories*.

1965   Publishes *Collected Poems, Love Respelt* (poetry), *Mammon and the Black Goddess* (lectures).

1968   Receives Queen's Gold Medal for Poetry, Cultural Olympics, Mexico City.

1969   Publishes *The Crane Bag*, poetry.

1970   Made Honorary Member, American Academy of Arts and Sciences.

1971   Publishes *Poems, 1968–1970*.

1977   *New Collected Poems* (his last published book to date).

1

Biography

"I had, by the age of twenty-three, been born, initiated into formal religion, travelled, learned to lie, loved unhappily, been married, gone to the war, taken life, procreated my kind, rejected formal religion, won fame, and been killed." So writes Robert Graves in his autobiography *Good-bye to All That*.[1] There is obviously more to the story, since, at this writing (1978), Robert Graves is eighty-three years old. The most recent book of an incredibly prolific career as poet, novelist, literary critic, biographer, lecturer, translator, and mythographer appeared only last year—poetry, of course, the most constant love of his life.

His immediate ancestors include country pastors and what Graves called "the first modern historian" (Leopold von Ranke) on his mother's side. On his father's side, he comes from a long line of rectors, deans, and bishops with an occasional doctor and soldier. His father, Alfred Percival Graves, was a Gaelic scholar and wrote poetry of a conventional sort.

Alfred Graves was a widower when he married Amalie von Ranke. Amalie was forty years old, Alfred forty-nine, when Robert was born in Wimbledon (outside of London) on July 24, 1895. According to Graves, the two-generation gap between his own age and his parents' actually promoted the most amicable relations between them.

Robert had a conventional Victorian home and upbringing. His father was away most of the time, as inspector

1

of schools for the Southwark district of London, or doing literary work or being president of literary or temperance societies. He was kind and playful with the children, however, on the occasional holidays. His mother was busy with the household and social obligations as wife of a public official. But it was hardly a lonely life. Robert had nine siblings, five of them from his father's first marriage. There were nurses to care for the children's needs.

The Graves household was religious, and Robert was a fervent evangelical Anglican until he was sixteen. At that time, he learned to his complete surprise that not everyone believed in Christ. It was the beginning of the end of his devout allegiance to Christianity.

His legacy from such early religious training was "a great capacity for fear, . . . a superstitious conscience and a sexual embarrassment." These lingered on to color later life long after the religious doctrine was discarded. He remained sentimentally attached, however, to the figure of Jesus as an ideal man.

Robert endured six different preparatory schools, accumulating unpleasant memories in each—at least, the ones he notes in his autobiography are usually frightening or humiliating. Though strongly attracted by the homosexuality that permeated the English public school system, his straight-laced upbringing kept him "honourably chaste and sentimental."

Up to age twelve, Robert and the other Graves children sometimes visited their grandfather and other relatives in Germany, including their aunt, Baronin von Aufsess, who lived in an imposing medieval castle in the Bavarian Alps. These fascinating environs no doubt influenced the boy's early romantic poetry.

Later, Robert's German connections were an embarrassment to him. When he entered Charterhouse preparatory school, he began to insist that he was Irish, after his father, who was Scotch on his mother's side, but Irish through his father. This thorough rejection of the German part of his heritage remained till the close of World War I.

At Charterhouse, Graves felt miserably out of place. Almost everyone despised school work; the chief interests were games and romantic attachments. Graves was always short of pocket money. Moreover, his name appeared on the school lists as "R. von R. Graves," when anti-German sentiment ran high. To avoid harrassment, he even faked insanity, after which nobody bothered him. Eventually he attained a certain respect from his classmates by becoming a competent boxer.

He was still at Charterhouse when he found a friend in George Mallory, famous mountaineer who later died on Everest. Mallory interested Edward Marsh in the poetry that Graves was writing. Marsh, then secretary to Winston Churchill, was a patron of the contemporary Georgian school of poetry. He encouraged Graves in his writing, but advised him to modernize his diction, which was forty years behind the times. Later in France, Graves became friends with the war poet Siegfried Sassoon, who also whetted his ambition to write poetry.

When World War I started, Graves joined the Royal Welsh Fusiliers and soon went to France as a nineteen-year-old officer. In his autobiography, written when he was thirty-five, he provides one of the best descriptions of trench warfare to come out of the war—a gritty, objective account of a soldier's daily life. One in three of his generation at school lost their lives. At some stages of the war, the average service of an infantry subaltern on the Western Front before death or incapacitating wounds was only about three months.

In 1916, Graves was seriously wounded by bursting shells. One piece of shell in the thigh almost emasculated him. Another split the bone of a finger, another lodged just above the eye. But the most dangerous wound was in the chest, narrowly missing his heart; the damage to his lungs lasted for years after the event. He lay in a coma for twenty-four hours. His commanding officer saw him and gave him up for dead. He put him on the casualty list and sent a letter of condolence to his mother. Graves lay immobile in a

neglected corner of a hospital tent while the battle raged on.
Finally someone noticed that the "corpse" had moved.
Four days later he was on a hospital train celebrating his
twenty-first birthday.

Graves suffered mental as well as physical wounds in
the war. Like many other victims, including his friend Sassoon, Graves came under the care of a prominent Cambridge neurologist and psychologist, W. H. R. Rivers. Rivers was a Freudian psychologist and a specialist in war
neurasthenia, popularly known as shell shock. He also was
very interested in the role of the subconscious in poetic
creation. Under his influence, Graves became fascinated
with the nature of dreams and their relationship to the creative imagination.

For ten years, however, Graves was inclined to night-
mares of bursting shells and waking hallucinations wherein
strangers looked like friends who had died in battle. When
he walked in the country in England or Wales, he would
find himself working on tactical problems. How would he
take that hill? What should he do in case of attack from the
sea? Where should he station the heavy guns? During this
period, much of his poetry was haunted by despair, guilt,
and images of entrapment.

Graves's wounds earned him only a temporary reprieve
from active military duty. He and Sassoon spent some time
together writing poetry and suggesting revisions of each other's poetry. They were both bitterly disillusioned about the
political realities of wartime Britain. "The view we had of
the war was now non-political," Graves wrote. "We no
longer saw it as a war between trade-rivals; its continuance
seemed merely a sacrifice of the idealistic younger generation to the stupidity and self-protective alarm of the elder."

Nevertheless, Graves returned to the front, but before
long he developed bronchitis and was brought back to train
officers at Somerville College.

Sassoon soon returned to England also, shot in the
throat. More bitter than ever, Sassoon published a con-

demnation of politicians for continuing the war. Although
Graves agreed with his friend in theory, he feared Sassoon
was not strong enough to take the court-martial and imprisonment which might result from this stand. Graves hurried
to forestall Sassoon's court-martial by pleading with the
medical board that Sassoon needed psychiatric treatment.
Graves was in such a state of shattered nerves himself at this
time that he burst into tears three times in his plea. Sassoon
was assigned to a convalescent home for neurasthenics.

Sassoon later returned to the front. He was shot in the
head while making a daylight patrol through long grass in
no man's land. Yet he survived this brush with death also.
"And he wrote me a verse letter which I cannot quote,
though I should like to do so." Graves wrote. "It is the most
terrible of his war-poems."

In January 1918, when he was twenty-two years old,
Graves married eighteen-year-old Nancy Nicholson,
painter, socialist, and vehement feminist. It must have been
a rather curious event. Nancy was furious when she realized
the sexist language of the marriage ceremony. Graves
characterized Nancy coolly in his autobiography as "ignorant, but independent-minded, good-natured, hard, and as
sensible about the war as anybody at home could be." The
wedding cake was covered with a plaster case that looked
like icing. There just wasn't enough sugar for the frosting.
During their wedding night bombs dropping not far off kept
the hotel in an uproar.

A week later Nancy returned to her farm and he to his
soldiers. When he was transferred to the Sixteenth Officer
Cadet Battalion at Rhyl from February 1918 to the armistice
in November, Nancy came to live with him and soon became pregnant.

Robert and Nancy had four children, two girls and two
boys—just as Nancy had planned it. It was an emancipated
household: Nancy painted, Robert wrote poetry, and they
shared the housework and child care. The boys took Graves's
last name; Nancy kept her maiden name and designated the

daughters' name as Nicholson. Graves even acted as midwife at one of the births. He was appalled at the pain and
general messiness of the process.

Graves and his family lived in a cottage on John
Masefield's estate and tried to become shopkeepers for a
while. The store lasted six months before collapsing finan-
cially, leaving the Graveses three hundred pounds in debt.
Nancy's father sent them one hundred pounds; the rest was
provided by one of Graves's new friends, T. E. Lawrence.
Lawrence gave Graves four chapters of *Seven Pillars of Wisdom*, a history of the Arabian revolt that Lawrence partici-
pated in, to sell in the United States. He had vowed to make
no money himself on the revolt, but thought it might help a
poet in financial difficulty. Graves later wrote a successful
biography of Lawrence and his Arabian exploits.

Graves met a great many other prominent figures in
England: Bertrand Russell, H. G. Wells, Aldous Huxley,
John Galsworthy, A. A. Milne, Thomas Hardy, Walter De
La Mare, T. S. Eliot, the Woolfs, the Sitwells. Although he
was publishing a volume of poetry himself every year between 1920 and 1925, it was a time of considerable depression. He was trying to exorcise some of his emotional problems through his poetry. Philosophical interests were
gradually pushing the psychological orientation into the
background, however, partly because of his stimulating contact with a Hindu, Basanto Mallik, who studied philosophy
at Oxford.

Nancy, meanwhile, was in poor health and needed a
change in climate. Graves decided he would have to take a
job to improve their finances. To that end, he completed
his thesis, published as *Poetic Unreason*, and got his
Bachelor of Letters degree at St. John's College in Oxford.
Then he obtained a position as professor of English literature at the new Egyptian University of Cairo—the only
salaried position he has ever held. He had been recommended by two friends, Arnold Bennett and T. E. Lawrence.

Accompanying Graves and his family to Egypt was a newfound friend, one who was to have a profound effect upon both Graves's personal life and his literary career. Both Robert and Nancy wanted her to stay with them. She was the American poet Laura Riding Gottschalk, a striking woman with a brilliant, original mind. She was the living embodiment of what Graves would later call his Goddess Muse.

Graves's marriage was already an unhappy one. Although Graves agreed with his wife's negative view of male domination, her extreme preoccupation with sexism was one of the elements that made their relationship uncomfortable. Concerning their socialist leanings, Graves wrote:

Socialism with Nancy was rather a means to a single end. The most important thing to her was judicial equality of the sexes; she held that all the wrong in the world was caused by male domination and narrowness. She refused to see my experience in the war as in any way comparable with the sufferings that millions of married women of the working class went through. This at least had the effect of putting the war into the background for me; I was devoted to Nancy and respected her views in so far as they were impersonal. Male stupidity and callousness became an obsession with her and she found it difficult not to include me in her universal condemnation of men.

The next year, Graves brought his household, including Laura, back to England and vowed henceforth to make his living by his writing alone.

Just what transpired in the domestic crisis that ensued is not entirely clear. Nancy and the four children apparently settled in a barge on the Thames; Robert and Laura in a flat not far away. Laura had already got a divorce from her American husband. Some unnamed person (one version says an Irish poet) was also staying at Graves's flat.

A heated altercation occurred between Laura and the unnamed poet (some say because the person in question preferred Nancy to Laura). Laura had a way of regarding all her associates as her property, owing her unquestioned allegiance. In any case, Laura became infuriated and leapt out of the fourth-story window. She survived with only a fractured spine, but spent the next three months in the hospital. Nancy and Robert parted company permanently at this time, and Robert became the faithful follower of Laura for the next thirteen years. A new phase of his life had begun.

It was a bitter time. Graves started writing his autobiography, partly because he needed money badly, partly to exorcise his painful past. *Good-bye to All That* marked an emotional watershed—"a story," he said, "of what I was, not what I am." It was an opportunity, he wrote at the beginning, for a "formal good-bye to you and to you and to you and to me and to all that; forgetfulness, because once all this has been settled in my mind and written down and published it need never be thought about again."

Graves's association with Laura Riding had considerable effect on his poetry. Riding was passionately interested in the meanings of words and sought truth, more than emotional expression, in poetry. She urged Graves to think more clearly, pursue verbal precision, and play down the emotional effects he used while he was still viewing poetry as psychologically therapeutic.

Graves and Riding eventually escaped the modern world, whose values they both despised, by settling in Déya, Majorca. Majorca was still relatively primitive at that time. Gertrude Stein had recommended it as "paradise, if you can stand it." Graves has lived in Majorca ever since, except during two wars that forced temporary evacuations.

The personal relationship between Graves and Riding was a curious one, with Laura playing the absolute queen, Robert serving cheerfully as her adoring consort. Laura's strange capacity to dominate a small group of associates receives considerable attention in a fascinating autobiographical narrative by T. S. Matthews, who knew them both. He considered Laura Riding and the poet Schuyler Jackson the most brilliant persons he had ever met.[2] According to

James McKinley in his introduction to Graves's last book, *New Collected Poems* (1977), Robert and Laura were lovers for a while, but later became friends and partners only.

After a hurried evacuation of British subjects from Spanish territory because of Franco's invasion, Graves and Riding moved about, living with various friends in England and Switzerland. In 1939, T. S. Matthews induced Laura and Robert to come to America and meet his friend, Schuyler Jackson, soon to become managing editor of *Time*. Matthews helped Jackson to remodel a big farmhouse Jackson owned in Pennsylvania. When it was ready, Schuyler Jackson, his wife Kit and their children, Graves and Riding, Matthews and his wife Julie, and another writer, Alan Hodge and his wife Beryl, all moved into the establishment. The household did not remain a big, happy family, however. Laura Riding, so used to ruling all around her, felt she had at last met her equal in Schuyler Jackson and fell in love with him. Jackson's wife suffered a nervous collapse under the strain. While Kit was in a sanitarium, Jackson finally divorced her in order to marry Laura. Robert, shattered by this turn of affairs, returned to England.

Graves was not long alone. Alan and Beryl Hodge soon joined him and another shift of allegiances took place, this time apparently with no ill feelings at all. Beryl moved in with Robert, while Alan and Robert collaborated amicably in writing the journalistic book *The Long Week-End. A Social History of Great Britain 1918–1939*. Beryl has been with Graves ever since. In 1946, Graves moved back to Majorca with Beryl and three children—a fourth was born to them in Majorca.

During this period Graves renewed his poetic creativity partly by his expanding awareness of ancient religions and mythologies. While doing research for a novel about Jason and the Golden Fleece, he became increasingly impressed with the pervasive pre-Achaean moon-goddess who seemed to dominate all early religious life. She appeared variously as nurturing mother, as seductive lover, as terrible death goddess. She was the center of wisdom and poetic inspiration. She bound men both to the seasons of nature and to the demands of the spirit. She was the Triple Muse and all poets sang in her name.

When Graves discovered a similar pattern in Celtic folklore and literature, and correlated the findings of such anthropologists as Robert Briffault, J. J. Bachofen, James Frazer, Jane Harrison, Margaret Murray,[3] and some of the recent discoveries in archaeology, he was convinced that the goddess cult once permeated the whole western world. Moreover, many of the ills of civilization stemmed from her overthrow and the subsequent male domination of religion and social values.

In this pattern of myth, which seemed so appropriate to his temperament and his experience, Graves found the unified vision he needed to animate his poetry for the rest of his life. He published this vision in *The White Goddess* (1948), a difficult, and to some exasperating, book. It has undoubtedly had a significant influence upon literature. With this and other works on myth, he is an important contributor to the current renewal of interest in ancient mythology and folklore.

Robert Graves, though he advocates a mythology wherein women are the spiritual leaders of men, has become a patriarch in his own time. He has seldom left Majorca again except to deliver lectures or to receive medals and honors. He has lectured at Oxford, at Trinity College, and Massachusetts Institute of Technology in Cambridge, in California, Hungary, Israel, and Spain. He became a controversial figure among academics with his unorthodox studies of Greek and Hebrew myth and his rewriting of the gospels. He did translations in several languages, wrote historical novels on the side, and produced a steady stream of poetry.

But quite aside from his forays into the outer world, young poets have pilgrimaged to Majorca for his advice and encouragement. With the demise of such fashionable movements as imagism and the diminishing force of T. S. Eliot and Ezra Pound as dictators to poetic taste, many younger poets have turned to Graves, the meticulous craftsman with words, who despised all schools and pre-determined formulas. Every true poem, Graves has taught them, is original not imitative, and each poem determines its own rhythm, diction, and form. This is good advice from an old master, who also happens to be the most persistent literary maverick of our time.

2

The White Goddess
and the Art of Poetry

Although *The White Goddess* is probably the most famous (or notorious) of his critical works, Graves has a long history of literary criticism. Some of it he has later disavowed. Some seems unnecessarily vicious in dealing with brilliant contemporaries, such as Yeats. (Is he so irritated with Yeats because he, too, created a private symbol system that rivals his own?) Yet Graves has a coherent theory of poetry, quite aside from his more arcane speculations about the relationship between ancient religious ritual and the poetic art. We will look first at some of the "pure" critical theory—pure, that is, in the sense of unencumbered by anthropological and mythological considerations.

In one of his Oxford lectures called "The Poet in a Valley of Dry Bone" (in *Mammon and the Black Goddess*, 1963), Graves has a particularly lucid explanation of the poetic process. The art of the poet is the result of long experience and attention to the meanings of words, a carefully developed craftsmanship, and an intuitive openness to what Graves calls the poetic trance. Though he started writing poems himself at age thirteen, he says there are no child prodigies in poetry, as there are in music. "A long, long experience with language is needed before words can fully collaborate with one another under the poetic trance. It seems necessary, too, to have read a great many poems by other writers, good and bad, before a poet can realize his powers and limitations."

The craftsmanship of poetry, Graves says, is self-taught. "A poet lives with his own language, continually instructing himself in the origin, histories, pronunciation, and peculiar usages of words, together with their latent powers, and the exact shades of distinction between what Roget's *Thesaurus* calls 'synonyms.'"

Some languages, such as French, have officially correct ways of expressing every thought, but English has only precedents. One needs to know the precedents and when it may be wise to create one's own precedent. Graves says that he consults the Oxford English Dictionary four or five times a day, checking the derivations of words, how their meanings have changed, who used them, in what contexts. "The exact rightness of words can be explained only in the context of a whole poem: each one being related rhythmically, emotionally, and semantically, to every other."

Graves rejects decorative elaborations that add nothing to meaning. In *5 Pens in Hand*, he proposes a game he calls "Cables" to test a poem for superfluous verbiage. Imagine you are short of cash and have to cable the *sense* of each verse. He then offers a twelve-word cable of the forty-three word first stanza of Wordsworth's "Solitary Reaper." But he defies anyone to save much money by converting to a cable-gram Shakespeare's "Full fathom five thy father lies/ Of his bones are coral made. . . ."

As previously mentioned, Graves scorns schools and movements in poetry. One does not write good poetry by imitating either a popular fashion or a real genius. The idea or experience one wishes to express should determine the form, the diction, the rhythm—and the style should always be the writer's own. "I never have much use for one whose poems I do not recognize at a glance as inimitably his own; even so, I reject them if they draw attention to a cultivated eccentricity, to pride in scholarship, or to the master of Classical or Modernist technique."

Technique, as used here, suggests a more mechanical process than the craftsmanship Graves favors. It is partly timing and emphasis that makes the difference. The master of technique may be more concerned with showing off his rhetorical skills than conveying a poetic message—like an orator who sounds impressive, but makes no sense. For Graves, a poem must make sense; deliberate obscurity is an affectation. (Graves condemns Ezra Pound on this score.) But the poem must begin "beyond reason" in inspiration, welling up from the poetic trance. After the initial rush of expression comes critical appraisal and meticulous rewriting, where all the poet's craft is put to the service of the unique requirements of this particular poem. Graves says he writes approximately ten drafts of a poem.

On the creative process in poetry, Graves writes, in *Mammon and the Black Goddess:*

The Vienna school of psychology presumes a conscious and unconscious mind, as two separate and usually warring entities, but a poet cannot accept this. In the poetic trance, he has access not only to the primitive emotions and thoughts which lie stored in his childhood memory, but to all his subsequent experiences— emotional and intellectual; including a wide knowledge of English won by constant critical study. Words are filed away by their hundred thousand, not in alphabetical order but in related groups; and as soon as the trance seizes him, he can single out most of the ones he needs. Moreover, when the first heavily blotted draft has been copied out fairly before he goes to bed, and laid aside for reconsideration, he will read it the next morning as if it were written by another hand. Yet soon he is back in the trance, finds that his mind has been active while he was asleep on the problem of internal relations, and that he can substitute the exact right word for the stand-in with which he had to be content the night before.

This illuminating description probably does not disprove the theory of the subconscious mind. It does suggest, however, that the skillful poet has remarkable access to buried memories and emotions, and to so much verbal aptitude that experience leaps out fully clothed in words. Lines of poetry that emerge spontaneously from trance will choose their own rhythm and suggest their own best form.

Graves described this poetic trance in some of his first critical works in the 1920s. His collected essays entitled *The Common Asphodel*, containing observations on poetry dated from 1922–1949 (some of which were collaborations with Laura Riding) begins with that topic:

The nucleus of every poem worthy of the name is rhythmically formed in the poet's mind, during a trance-like suspension of his normal habits of thought, by the supra-logical reconciliation of conflicting emotional ideas. The poet learns to induce the trance in self-protection whenever he feels unable to resolve an emotional conflict by simple logic.... As soon as he has... dissociated himself from the poem, the secondary phase of composition begins: that of testing and correcting on commonsense principles, so as to satisfy public scrutiny, what began as a private message to himself from himself—yet taking care that nothing of poetic value is lost or impaired. For the reader of the poem must fall into a complementary trance if he is to appreciate its full meaning. The amount of revision needed depends largely on the strength and scope of the emotional disturbance and the degree of trance.

Graves goes on to say that the critical sense is not completely suspended in light trance. Some trances are so deep, however, that the poem evoked is close to dream, wherein thought connections are governed by free association and the atmosphere charged with emotions the writer himself may not understand. (This observation, one might note, suggests that there is, indeed, a subconscious mind.) The classic example of dream poetry is Samuel Taylor Coleridge's "Kubla Khan."

Graves did not, in his earlier career, speak disparagingly of Freud. When he was struggling with his war-neurosis, under the care of Dr. Rivers, Graves thought that the writing of poetry could be psychologically therapeutic. The insight gained during his protracted illness and treatment, as he says specifically in *Poetic Unreason* and *On English Poetry*, helped him to develop an aesthetic for the next ten years, until he came under the influence of Laura Riding.

Daniel Hoffman has analyzed the contribution of Dr. Rivers to Graves's aesthetic in *Barbarous Knowledge*. Hoffman quotes Rivers's *Conflict and Dream*, then explains that Graves derived support from Rivers for these convictions:

First, the poem, like the dream, is a symbolic presentation and resolution of individual emotional conflicts. Graves holds this conception still, although he has modified an accompanying theorem he held in the 1920's that the chief value of poetry is therapeutic.

Rivers's second point of use to Graves is that there is the *materia poetica* ('the unelaborated product of the poet's mind') which is subjected to 'a lengthy process of a critical kind, comparable with ... the secondary elaboration of the dream.' Hence the completed poem requires the collaboration of both the intuitive and the critical faculties of the mind. ...

From Rivers's statement that 'the real underlying meaning or latent content of the poem' is in fact quite different from that suggested by its outward imagery, Graves takes warrant for a reading of the poetry of others that can only be called idiosyncratic. And finally, the assertion ... that only the poet himself can reveal 'the real mechanism of artistic production' [as the individual is the best interpretor of his own dreams] leads Graves to deduce universal principles of poetry from the analysis of his own practice.[1]

One of these universal laws of poetics that Graves derives from his own experience, as Hoffman points out, is that there is no such thing as a true long poem. Poems should be devoted to a single subject—a principle also advanced by Edgar Allan Poe. That is one, though by no means the only, reason Graves is harsh with Milton. Again, Graves is not much interested in verse drama, even Shakespeare's, except for the isolated poems that can be extracted from them. As Hoffman implies, Graves seems to have limited tolerance for kinds of poetry that seem foreign to his own practice.

In 1927, Graves collaborated with Laura Riding on *A Survey of Modernist Poetry*. It contains a perceptive discus-

sion of modern methods of poetry, using such innovators as
Cummings and Eliot, as well as some excellent comments
on older poems, especially Shakespearean sonnets. It
analyzes the reasons for and shortcomings of faddish
movements in poetry, such as imagism and Georgianism.
Dead movements, they explain, are focused on the problem
of style. Yet every poem should be a "new and self-
explanatory creature," dictating its own style.

Both Graves and Riding are known for their caustic
judgments on poets whose methods they dislike. The work
of the imagist poet H. D. (Hilda Doolittle), for instance, is
"so thin, so poor, that its emptiness seemed 'perfection,' its
insipidity to be concealing a 'secret,' its superficiality so 'gla-
cial' that it created a false 'classical' atmosphere." Of Gertrude Stein, ". . . she was only divinely inspired in ordinari-
ness: her creative originality, that is, was original only because it was so grossly, so humanly, all-inclusively ordinary.
She used language automatically to record pure ultimate
obviousness." (One can't help thinking of the "pop art"
painting of a huge Campbell's soup can.)

Modern experimental poetry, Graves and Riding say,
has been influenced by nonrepresentational art—especially
in the abandonment of meter. But poetry is necessarily
linked with metrical forms designed to create in the reader a
hypersensitive awareness of meaning. Verse forms are not
rigid; they accommodate considerable stress and variation.
But to discard them entirely, as in free verse, is to abandon a
major requirement of the poetic mood.

The change from meter to free verse occurred around
1911, when English poetry was at low ebb. It became fashionable for the poet, modeling himself after the nonrepresentational artist, to abandon coherent statement, but to
create abstract arrangements of emotionally laden phrases
and sounds. In "Legitimate Criticism of Poetry" in *5 Pens
in Hand*, Graves praises John Crowe Ransom and Robert
Frost as true masters of experimental form, adapting individual speech rhythm and diction to conventional verse
forms, as Shakespeare did.

In a comment in 1949, when Graves republished some of his collaborations with Laura Riding in *The Common Asphodel,* he made some gloomy predictions on the fate of poets in the modern world. True poets literally have no place to go and little audience except each other. That, of course, is one reason Graves fled the modern world to the relatively primitive and remote Majorca.

The Communist state demands verse which glorifies national achievement under the Marxist theory and shows a complete divorce from European literary models; the big-business state demands verse which soothes the vanity and condones the near-illiteracy of the Hollywood-educated populace. . . . The writing of poems is therefore likely to become a more private affair than ever.

Most poets, he says in *Food for Centaurs,* gravitate to the teaching profession, where they may be able to write some poems, at least on vacations. Yet this is the "most damaging of all professions for a poet." There are just too many obligations and restrictions that fritter away his mental and emotional substance.

He must not diverge from the curriculum; he must teach a great many things which he knows to be useless, boring, or even untrue; he must discipline his pupils; he must pretend to know the answer to every question; he must lead a life secure against moral objection even from the most narrow-minded critic.

Under the circumstances, a poet apparently ought to be independently wealthy or, like Graves, produce some more popular forms of literature on the side.

Graves's *magnum opus, The White Goddess,* which he calls "A Historical Grammar of Poetic Myth," is so complex a document that it almost defies analysis. Even a reader fairly knowledgeable in myth can become mired in the voluminous details and lose the thread of the argument. Although the book is obviously a synthesis of all his research and meditation on ancient religions, the purpose of poetry, and a traditional body of literature, Graves says his argument is based on a detailed examination of two Welsh

minstrel poems of the thirteenth century, *Câd Goddeu* and
Hanes Taliesin, which ingeniously conceal the clues to an
ancient secret.

He summarizes his findings in the Foreword:

My thesis is that the language of poetic myth anciently current in
the Mediterranean and Northern Europe was a magical language
bound up with popular religious ceremonies in honour of the
Moon-goddess, or Muse, some of them dating from the Old Stone
Age, and that this remains the language of true poetry—'true' in
the nostalgic modern sense of 'the unimprovable original, not a
synthetic substitute'. The language was tampered with in late Mi-
noan times when invaders from Central Asia began to model or
falsify the myths to justify the social changes. Then came the early
Greek philosophers who were strongly opposed to magical poetry
as threatening their new religion of logic, and under their influence a rational poetic language (now called the Classical) was
elaborated in honour of their patron Apollo and imposed on the
world as the last word in spiritual illumination: a view that has
prevailed practically ever since in European schools and universities, where myths are now studied only as quaint relics of the
nursery age of mankind.

The secret hidden in the Welsh minstrel poems involves an esoteric tree alphabet used by wandering bards,
the master-poets of Wales. When the country became
Christianized, the bards tried to express the traditional
pagan theme of bardic poetry in terms so disguised that the
Church could not accuse them of heresy. They did this,
presumably, with puzzling riddles and the ancient symbolism of the tree alphabet, which the Christians did not
know.

The Theme, briefly, is the antique story, which falls into thirteen
chapters and epilogue, of the birth, life, death and resurrection of
the God of the Waxing Year; the central chapters concern the
God's losing battle with the God of the Waning Year for love of the
capricious and all-powerful Threefold Goddess, their mother,
bride and layer-out. The poet identifies himself with the God of
the Waxing Year and his Muse with the Goddess; the rival is his
blood-brother, his other self, his weird.

The God of the Waxing Year is, of course, a variation of the primitive vegetation god. He revives in the spring but suffers death in the fall, like the Egyptian Osiris, murdered by his brother Set, god of desert and drouth, only to be restored by his wife Isis. The poet sees himself in both creative and sacrificial roles, alternately inspired by the love of the Goddess Muse and suffering ritual death when her love grows cold.

Graves first found what is called the Beth-Luis-Nion tree alphabet in seventeenth century Roderick O'Flaterty's *Ogygia*. O'Flaterty presented it as a genuine relic of the Druids, who used it for divination. Graves has the decency to warn us that he wrote to Dr. Macalister, "the best living authority on Oghams," who told him not to take O'Flaterty's alphabet seriously. Nevertheless, Graves does do so, insisting that the clue to understanding seemingly nonsensical riddles in the *Romance of Taliesin* lies in knowing the secret tree alphabet, which was correlated to a tree calendar.

The alphabet has five vowels and thirteen consonants. Each letter is named after a tree or shrub. Graves explains the mythological associations that surround each tree symbolized in a letter. *H*, for instance, is the ash, sacred to Poseidon, also to Woden, or Wotan, or Odin, or Gwidion (as it was variously written), who uses it as his steed in "The Battle of the Trees," a poem in *Câd Goddeu*. But *H* was originally associated with the Scandinavian Triple Goddess, who dispensed justice under the ash tree.

F is the alder, the tree of Bran. *S* is the willow, sacred to Hecate, Circe, Hera, and Persephone, all death aspects of the Triple Goddess. *D* is the oak, "the tree of Zeus, Jupiter, Hercules, The Dagda (the chief of the older Irish gods), Thor, and all other thunder gods, Jehovah in so far as he was 'El,' and Allah." This is the sacred oak that Sir James Frazer elucidated at such length in *The Golden Bough*.

Graves's remarks on the letter *T* illustrate his capacity for intuitive synthesis, which some may regret as untrustworthy. Whether or not it says something reliable about how people perceive Jesus, it does illuminate one of the great English classics, *Sir Gawain and the Green Knight*.

The eighth tree is the holly, which flowers in July. The holly appears in the originally Irish *Romance of Gawain and the Green Knight*. The Green Knight is an immortal giant whose club is a holly-bush. He and Sir Gawain, who appears in the Irish version as Cuchulain, a typical Hercules, make a compact to behead one another at alternate New Years—meaning midsummer and midwinter—but when it comes to the point, the Holly Knight spares the Oak Knight. Since in medieval practice St. John, who lost his head on St. John's day, took over the oak-king's titles and customs, it was natural to let Jesus, as John's merciful successor, take over the holly-king's. The holly was thus glorified beyond the oak.

Thus, the medieval bard, versed in an ancient pagan tradition, would tell the Christ story as another version of the birth, death, and resurrection of the God of the Waxing Year. Later in the discussion, however, Graves regrets the association of Jesus with the holly as poetically inept. ". . .It was the oak-king, not the holly-king, who was crucified on a T-shaped cross."

"The Battle of the Trees" in *Câd Goddeu* is a perfect example of what Graves calls "mythographic shorthand," which "records what seems to have been the most important religious event in pre-Christian Britain." Though the action involves only anthropomorphized trees and shrubs, the subject of this legend, Graves tells us, is a battle for religious mastery between the armies of Dôn, "the folk of the God whose mother is Danu," and the armies of Arawn ("Eloquence"), the King of Annwfn, the British underworld or city of the dead. In other words, it celebrates the supplanting of one priesthood and cult by another.

As soon as one has mastered the elementary grammar and the accidence of myth, and built up a small vocabulary, and learned to distinguish seasonal myths from historical and iconotropic myths, one is surprised how close to the surface lie the explanations, lost since pre-Homeric times, of legends that are still religiously conserved as part of our European cultural inheritance.

All this lore about archaic alphabets and solar and lunar calendars seems to be evidence of a mythographic frame of reference that permeated a more poetic age wherein the Great Goddess was supreme. The book explores a prodigious range of such evidence covering northern and southern Europe, north Africa, and the Middle East.

When J. M. Cohen sent the typescript of his critical appraisal to Robert Graves for approval, Graves made notes in the margin. Cohen had written in reference to *The White Goddess*: "But the work is never for a moment a work of scholarship."[2] Graves wrote the following mild comment beside this remark: "The odd thing is that it is becoming more and more accepted by serious historians and anthropologists and the flaw in the argument, if there is one, has never been found."

As a matter of fact, much of what Graves says about the widespread worship of the Great Goddess can be verified in a volume of impeccable scholarship: *The Cult of the Mother Goddess* by E. O. James.[3] James makes no reference whatever to Graves, though he does mention in a footnote the psychological approach of Erich Neumann in *The Great Mother*.[4] Actually, the idea is not new, having been proposed in the nineteenth century by certain anthropologists, particularly J. J. Bachofen in *Myth, Religion & Mother Right*, originally published in German, but translated in 1967 for Princeton University Press. The James book, however, is undoubtedly less speculative and less biased by value judgments than Bachofen's.

Bachofen believed, as Graves does, that matriarchal forms of social structure preceded patriarchal ones, a notion in far more doubt among scholars than the existence of goddess cults. In some circumstances, Graves uses the term matrilinear, which is more easily argued than that political power rested in women. Matrilinear refers only to line of descent through the mother, not the father. It does not necessarily mean that the clan would be ruled in practical and political matters by women. Graves says that Samson's leaving his own clan to join Delilah indicates a matriarchal arrangement. Also, in the Garden of Eden story, Adam says "Therefore shall a man leave his father and his mother, and shall cleave unto his wife." Yet, in a patriarchal clan system, it is the woman, not the man, who must leave father and mother to cleave to her husband. For more detailed discussion of the anthropological aspects of this controversy, see the next chapter devoted to mythology.

The most idiosyncratic part of Graves's message, however, is not that society was once matrilinear or that goddess-worship once existed and inspired poets, but that goddess-worship is even now the only source of inspiration for the "true" poet. That is why, as already noted, Graves considers the modern world, dominated by business, politics, science, and technology—in other words, "Apollonian reason"—to be a barren wasteland for poetry.

With this remarkable book, Graves gathered from multiple streams of thought, a reservoir of ideas, metaphors, and images that he has used ever since in poetry and even in fiction. He has remained primarily a love poet, since the poet identifies with the God of the Waxing Year, regarding the Queen with mingled love and dread. This orientation undoubtedly initiated a burst of creative achievement. It may be, however, that it has limited the scope of his work in the long run. Some of his earlier poems on psychological and philosophical subjects are at least the equal of his Goddess poems. Moreover, some of his latest poems seem repetitive, as though he had run out of original ways to tell the "one story only." But he did find an appropriate fair haven for his talent, which allowed his essentially romantic nature to stay young and vigorous into old age. He has certainly proved that romanticism need not be cloyed with sentimentalism and stock phrases.

Graves must be at least partially responsible for renewed contemporary interest in myth in a number of academic fields. His complaint at the beginning of *The White Goddess* that myths are now studied only as "quaint relics of the nursery age of mankind" no longer seems accurate. Curiously, one concentration of interest in the subject is in Jungian psychology, an orientation he openly despised. Perhaps he "doth protest too much," since Jungian psychology could probably offer a rather credible explanation of Graves's obsession with the White Goddess.

In the Jungian conception of the subconscious the *anima*, the feminine element in a man's nature, has a function somewhat analogous to the Muse. It presumably may communicate to the conscious mind some of the knowledge that normally lies buried in the subconscious (which Graves claims he doesn't have). This energy is personified in men's dreams, the Jungians tell us, sometimes as young girl, sometimes as alluring woman, sometimes as terrifying hag. *The White Goddess*, both in historical belief and in Graves himself, might thus be a projection of a psychological archetype. (Whether there are such things as animas and archetypes, I do not pretend to know. That there are *literary* archetypes is more demonstrable.)

Nevertheless, Graves has had a salubrious effect upon poetry, insisting upon both inspiration and craftsmanship, ridiculing cliché and insincerity, promoting a meticulous study of the meanings and emotional overtones of words. These values will surely always be valid. Moreover, for the "now" generation, he demonstrates that even the remote past may impart some unique wisdom to the perceptive mind.

3

The White Goddess
and *The Greek Myths*

Who is the White Goddess? She is the first deity of the ancient world—Mother Night, Homer called her, of whom even the gods stand in awe. She is the archetypal female trinity: Mother, Siren, and Witch, who presides over birth, love, and death. She is the Three Fates who spin out a man's life and cut the thread, and the Three Norns of Scandinavian legend who stand under the ash tree and mete out justice.

She is Leucothea, Pelasgian mother-goddess, and Albino, or Alphito, who gave her name to Britain (Albion), and the Goddess Eire, who gave her name to Ireland. She is Semele, goddess of the moon, mother of Dionysius, and Great Egyptian Isis, mother of Horus, and Hathor, and Astarte, and Themis, whom the anthropologist Jane Harrison called "the social imperative that constitutes religion."[1] She is Demeter, the Barley-goddess of primitive Greece, and Core *alias* Persephone *alias* Proserpine, her daughter, who rules the underworld, as the Goddess Erishkigal does in the Sumerian *Epic of Gilgamesh*. She is the Sumerian Ma, "mother," *alias* Mari of Cyprus, *alias* Marienna, "fruitful mother of Heaven," *alias* Miriam, *alias* Marion, *alias* Myrrhine, *alias* Mariamne, and Anna, to Christian mystics "God's Grandmother."

She is Artemis *alias* Diana, Goddess of the moon and wild things. She is the witch Hecate, goddess of the dark of the moon, and Circe and Calypso and Leucippe, the White

Mare. She is Choere or Phorcis, the White Sow. She is
Hera, Zeus's wife, who was originally a death goddess having charge of the souls of sacred kings and making oracular
heroes of them.

She is Aphrodite *alias* Venus, who in Syria and Pales-
tine was Ashtoroth or Ishtar *alias* Inanna of the *Epic of
Gilgamesh*. She is Cybele, the lion-and-bee goddess of
Phrygia, and Brigit, the British Triple Goddess of Poetry,
Healing, and Smithcraft, whom the Roman Catholics obligingly turned into a saint. She is Io, the White Cow, and
Cerridwen, the cat and sow-goddess of Wales, and Aruru,
the Babylonian "Bright Mother of the Hollow" who created
everything, and Tiamat the Sea-serpent whom Marduk defeated, and Rahab the Sea-goddess, who becomes in the
Bible Rahab-the-Harlot, and the Great Goddess Danu, who
evolved into a masculine Donnus or Dôn and possibly Dis,
a universal god analogous to Jehovah. (This is the pagan
deity which Margaret Murray in *The God of the Witches*
says was the real focus of worship in medieval witch cults,
not the Christian devil.)

She has many other names: Belili, Sumerian mother-
goddess, later masculinized into Bel, and Pasiphaë, Cretan
moon-goddess, and Danaë of Argos, and Cotytto or Cotys,
worshipped both in northern Britain and in Thrace,
Corinth, and Sicily, and Eurynome, the Goddess of All
Things who rose naked from original Chaos, and Cardea
and Mother Rhea, and Carmento, the Italian Triple Muse,
and Morgan le Faye, King Arthur's sister. Graves has even
hinted that Eve's title, "the Mother of All Living," belonged
originally to the pagan Great Goddess, and that the reason
for the rise of the Virgin Mary cult in the Middle Ages was
the uncommon persistence of goddess worship.

Should this attribute of whiteness seem inconsistent
with a goddess often associated with bloody sacrifice and
death, Graves explains in *The White Goddess*:

I write of her as the White Goddess because white is her principal
colour, the colour of the first member of her moon-trinity, but

when Suidas the Byzantine records that Io was a cow that changed her colour from white to rose and then to black he means that the New moon is the white goddess of birth and growth; the Full Moon, the red goddess of love and battle; the Old Moon, the black goddess of death and divination.

Besides that, the whiteness is not just the color of a woman's skin, but the dead white of the moon's face, often likened to the pallor of leprosy. She was described by Coleridge in *The Ancient Mariner* as the woman on the phantom ship who diced with Death for the mariner's life. She appears here in exactly the guise that Graves often uses:

> Her lips were red, her looks were free,
>   Her locks were yellow as gold,
> Her skin was white as leprosy,
> The Nightmare Life-in-Death was she,
>   Who thicks man's blood with cold.

The supremacy of goddesses arose in primitive times, presumably because of the ignorance of biological facts and the commonsense observation that only women could bring forth young. The first lasting social bond was not between sexual mates, but between mother and son. Therefore, the earliest social obligations were defined by women— analogous, perhaps, to what the Greek dramatists called the Ordinances of the Earth, the violation of which brought forth from the underworld the terrible female avengers, the Erinyes, or Furies.

When men deduced the fact of fatherhood, they began to assert their dominance over religious and clan rules. At times, they even went to a superficially logical extreme and decided that the seed of life was entirely in male semen. Woman was only a "vessel" to receive it—a view implicit in the Bible and explicit in Apollo's defense of Orestes in Aeschylus' *Eumenides*. Orestes escaped the ravages of the Furies, even though he committed the blackest crime of the more ancient matriarchal society—killing his own mother. Apollo (the god of truth?) claimed that only fathers were parents! The presiding judge, Athene, who originally was

the Libyan Triple Goddess Neith (by the Greeks called
Lamia or Libya), had been reborn of Zeus's head. She
therefore voted for Orestes, since she was now "all for the
Father."

As Graves states in his introduction to *The Greek
Myths:*

A study of Greek mythology, as Bachofen and Briffault insisted
long ago, should begin with an understanding of the matriarchal
and totemistic system which obtained in Europe before the arrival
of patriarchal invaders from the east and north. One can then
follow its gradual supersession first by a matrilineal and then by a
patrilineal sacred monarchy, at last by a fully patriarchal
system—as the migrant tribe with its phratries and clans gave place
to the regional state with its towns and villages.

With these generalizations as basic assumptions, then,
Graves assembles the Greek myths in two volumes, so that
they make a continuous narrative, beginning with creation
stories and ending with Odysseus's wanderings. He follows
each separate narrative with historical or anthropological
observations, comparative notations to analogous mythical
events, and odd remnants of the belief in present day customs. These speculative and scholarly observations are
clearly differentiated from the myth itself and from each
other. Everything is carefully indexed so that references to a
given mythological personage may be traced to all references to that figure. The sources of the myths, or particular
portions of them, are footnoted after each story. Variants of
the myth follow the main narrative. *The Greek Myths* is a
peculiarly vital and coherent account, and a pleasure to
read.

Graves believes that myths arise from different sources.
"True myth may be defined as the reduction to narrative
shorthand of ritual mime performed on public festivals, and
in many cases recorded pictorially on temple walls, vases,
seals, bowls, mirrors, chests, shields, tapestries, and the
like." This is the ritual approach, also entertained by Jane

Harrison, who, with James Frazer, was probably a significant influence on Graves's thinking.[2]

But Graves also insists that a large part of Greek myth is
politico-religious history. Often it is either the rationaliza-
tion of changes in religious allegiance, or perhaps simply
misreading the religious significance of icons belonging to a
conquered people. Thus, when patriarchal tribes from the
north overpowered the matriarchal civilization, the conquering chieftains, as representative of their male gods,
married the priestesses of the Goddess. "All early myths
about the gods' seduction of nymphs refer apparently to
marriages between Hellenic chieftains and local Moon-
priestesses, bitterly opposed by Hera, which means by con-
servative religious feeling." Mythologically speaking many
of these are recorded as rapes (Io, Danaë, Leto, Europa),
by Zeus. Other aspects of the Goddess (Artemis, Athene,
Aphrodite) are reduced to being Zeus's daughters.

Herbert Weisinger in *The Agony and the Triumph*[3]
accuses Graves of confused methodology because of this
double standard for myths. Graves promotes a monomyth,
on the one hand, a single pattern of death and rebirth in
obedience to the Goddess, but claims an historical basis for
those myths that don't fit the pattern. Weisinger claims that
other proponents of the ritual school deny that myth *ever*
originates in historical events or people, but freed from their
ritual origins may attach themselves to such events. Is this
origin of myth another "chicken-and-egg" problem? Or
perhaps a classification problem arising from the difficulty
of distinguishing legend from myth at this distance? It seems
to a nonprofessional to be too gray an area for such scholarly
precision.

Weisinger, himself, has a Freudian view quite similar,
perhaps, to the one Graves once entertained, but subsequently rejected. Weisinger writes:

I am fully persuaded that the mythopoeic mind, which stretches in
an unbroken line from the myth and ritual pattern of the ancient

Near East to the poet at work at his desk today, and which is as the
iceberg to its surfaced tip, can be understood only in terms of the
dream-work. I regret that many students of myth tend to look down
on Freud as an intruder in their field, but they forget that the
union of anthropology and psychoanalysis, which is the founda-
tion upon which the modern study of myth now rests, was sealed
by Freud; he was among the very first to grasp the significance of
Frazer's work from which he audaciously drew the conclusions
which Frazer either did not see or did not dare to express.[4]

Graves also claims to draw conclusions from James Frazer's
The Golden Bough that Frazer feared to reveal, especially in
regard to the striking similarity between Christ and the
pagan dying and resurrecting gods.

While Weisinger seems disturbed that Graves does not
consider the psychological undertones of myth, Joseph
Campbell, one of the leading mythologists with a Jungian
orientation, projects a view of ancient religion strikingly
similar to Graves's:

Now in the neolithic village stage of this development and dispersal, the focal figure of all mythology and worship was the bountiful
goddess Earth, as the mother and nourisher of life and receiver of
the dead for rebirth. In the earliest period of her cult (perhaps c.
7500–3500 B.C. in the Levant) such a mother-goddess may have
been thought of only as a local patroness of fertility, as many
anthropologists suppose. However, in the temples even of the first
of the higher civilizations (Sumer, c. 3500–2350 B.C.), the Great
Goddess of highest concern was certainly much more than that.
She was already, as she is now in the Orient, a metaphysical
symbol: the arch personification of the power of Space, Time, and
Matter, within whose bound all beings arise and die: the substance
of their bodies, configurator of their lives and thoughts, and receiver of their dead. And everything having form or name—
including God personified as good or evil, merciful or
wrathful—was her child, within her womb.

Toward the close of the Age of Bronze and, more strongly,
with the dawn of the Age of Iron (c. 1250 B.C. in the Levant), the
old cosmology and mythologies of the goddess mother were radically transformed, reinterpreted, and in large measure even sup-

pressed, by those suddenly intrusive patriarchal warrior tribesmen whose traditions have come down to us chiefly in the Old and New Testaments and in the myths of Greece.[5]

In spite of the supposed mutual exclusiveness of different theories of myth origins, however, in *The Greek Myths* Graves uses the ritualist Jane Harrison to illustrate a historical viewpoint:

Jane Harrison has pointed out (*Prolegomena to the Study of Greek Religion*, chapter v) that Medusa was once the goddess herself, hiding behind a prophylactic Gorgon mask: a hideous face intended to warn the profane against trespassing on her Mysteries. Perseus beheads Medusa: that is, the Hellenes overran the goddess's chief shrines, stripped her priestesses of their Gorgon masks, and took possession of the sacred horses[6]—an early representation of the goddess with a Gorgon's head and a mare's body has been found in Boeotia.

Jane Harrison certainly did not claim a matriarchal beginning for society, however. She believed that the first social structure was a strong male with his wives. The father killed or ran out the young males until he grew old or otherwise weak. Then the sons killed or maimed him. This scenario, incidentally, happens to fit neatly the pattern of antagonism and rebellion displayed in the succession of chief gods from Uranus, who was castrated by his son Cronus, who was thrown into Tartarus by his son Zeus, who quelled a rebellion among his own offspring. One is certainly tempted to account for such myths as recording a common social pattern in primitive times.

Graves suggests both ritual and historical sources for this grim succession of familial conflicts. He says Hesiod's version of the castration of Uranus by Cronus, aided and abetted by his sibling Titans and their Mother Earth, may reflect an early pre-Hellenic war between Titan-worshippers of central and southern Greece and early Hellenic invaders from the north. "The castration of Uranus is not necessarily metaphorical if some of the victors had originated in East

Africa where, to this day, Galla warriors carry a miniature sickle into battle to castrate their enemies; there are close affinities between East African religious rites and those of early Greece."

The dethronement of Cronus after he had swallowed all his children except Zeus, who is hidden by his mother Rhea, is explained as both historical and ritualistic in significance. The original ritual pattern was to sacrifice the Sacred King each fall, that he might be reborn in the spring. "But, by the times to which these myths refer, kings had been permitted to prolong their reigns to a Great Year of one hundred lunations, and offer annual boy victims in their stead; hence Cronus is pictured as eating his own sons to avoid dethronement." Zeus presumably outlived the subservience of the Sacred King to the vegetative rites of the Mother Goddess.

In spite of her description of the male-dominated primitive clan, Jane Harrison does confirm Graves's idea of matrilinear succession, at least in Crete, and the religious preeminence of women:

The cult of the Kouretes was at home in Crete and the great central worship of the Mother goddess. In the bridal chamber . . . of Crete the young men, before they might win their earthly brides, were initiated to the Mountain Mother and became symbolically her consorts or husbands. . . . Thus it will be seen that the Kouretes reflect a matrilinear social structure, the condition that naturally arises when parentage is precarious and often untraceable. Such a social structure focuses its attention on Mother and Child rather than on Father.[7]

Probably Graves's most convincing support, however, comes from modern archeology, not nineteenth century anthropology such as Frazer, Bachofen, or even Harrison, some of which is in disrepute. Even modern psychological approaches, such as Erich Neumann's *The Great Mother*, probably have only limited acceptance (and presumably none at all from Graves.) E. O. James, however, uses archeological sources for *The Cult of the Mother Goddess*.

He, too, describes a matrilinear cultural arrangement. He does not say that the Goddess-worshipping culture was initially matriarchal, but he says it is not at all improbable.[8] Certainly the Goddess was pre-eminent over her male consort, son, or lover. In the Preface, James writes:

Whether or not the Mother-goddess was the earliest manifestation of the concept of Deity, her symbolism unquestionably has been the most persistent feature in the archaeological record of the ancient world, from the sculptured Venuses of the Gravettian culture in the Upper Palaeolithic and the stylized images of the decorated caves, to the emblems and inscriptions of the cult when it became established in the Fertile Crescent, Western Asia, the Indus Valley, the Aegean and Crete between the fifth and third millennia B.C. Moreover, it is now becoming increasingly evident that in its dispersal from its cradleland in the Southern Russian steppe and Western Asia, it was destined to have a widespread influence and to play a very significant role in the subsequent development of the Ancient Near Eastern religions from India to the Mediterranean from Neolithic times to the Christian era.[9]

Some critics of *The Greek Myths* have claimed that it is not a scholarly synthesis at all, in the way it pretends, but a literary one, using purely literary conventions. Jay Macpherson, who also brings this charge against *King Jesus* and *The Nazarene Gospel Restored*, writes:

There is, actually, nothing genuinely primitive about the figure whom Graves celebrates: on the contrary, she is the very sophisticated product of a syncretism like the kind which was a regular principle of myth-interpretation from Alexandrian scholarship down to the time of Macrobius and after. A striking example Graves likes to quote is the speech of Isis in the *Metamorphoses* of Apuleius, which identifies her with some ten assorted cult-figures, and ultimately with the waxing and waning Moon as representing the eternal principle of generation and decay, or Nature herself. He accepts this account as the most adequate description in literature of his White Goddess, as it is certainly the most comprehensive. He goes farthest, apart from ritual matters like the system of sacred kingship in Greece, in making the Goddess the creatrix of the world. Neither Greek nor Semitic myth has this feature, though a case might be made for a female "dragon that is in the sea" as the ultimate origin of matter: Greek myth, mostly late, has world-eggs, but no world-hens or primeval she-doves, and Graves has had to concoct his account not only *ab ovo* but from before it. [10]

Granted that the evidence from a prehistoric age is very much harder to evaluate than later literature, still archeology offers more evidence than Mr. Macpherson seems willing to consider. This is not to say that Graves has not leaned heavily on later literature for his inferences about more primitive religion. Moreover, he no doubt improvised at times where evidence was thin. Nevertheless Joseph Campbell schematizes the evolution of creation myths almost exactly as Graves has:

1. the world born of a goddess without consort;
2. the world born of a goddess fecundated by a consort;
3. the world fashioned from the body of a goddess by a male warrior-god; and
4. the world created by the unaided power of a male god alone. [11]

Some myths, Graves contends, arise from accidental or deliberate misinterpretation of a sacred picture or rite, a process Graves calls "iconotropy." The so-called "Judgment of Paris," presumably deduced from an icon, is one instance. The prevailing myth says that the young shepherd has been asked to judge a beauty contest between Athene, Aphrodite, and Hera. He is handing an apple to the fairest. Paris chooses Aphrodite because she has bribed him with an offer of the most beautiful woman in the world (Helen). This scene, says Graves, is really the Triple Goddess (Athene the maid, Aphrodite the nymph, Hera the crone) presenting the hero with the apple, symbolizing her love bought at the price of his life. It will be Paris's passport to "the apple orchards of the west," that is, the Elysian Fields. Only the souls of heroes go there. He says this rite is analogous to the gift of an apple the Three Hesperides made to Heracles, and Eve, "the Mother of All Living" made to Adam.

Although Graves's critics seem to consider his controversial work only from the limited view of their own special-
ties, I wish that Graves too had kept his mind open to other
possibilities, especially the psychological elements of some
myths. One can only wonder if the struggle to put his
frightening war neurosis behind him forever did not induce
him to reject completely the psychoanalytic approach associated with that painful period. In this, Apollonian reason
triumphs and the nonrational becomes rationalized as displaced history. Graves is a strange combination of stubborn
commonsense and poetic, romantic intuition.

Scholars have an irresistible impulse to reduce very
complex data about human beings to one or a few universal
principles. Perhaps they envy the clarity of an Einstein, who
was inspired by the relative simplicity and universality of
basic physical laws of nature. Such lucidity, attractive as it
may be to the struggling intellect, may simply distort the
confusing study of mythology. Graves is not *necessarily*
wrong for pushing both ritualist and euhemerist approaches.
Perhaps, indeed, a great many other approaches are also
valid for *some* myths. Myths were not designed with an eye
to their ease of classification. Perhaps the sanest, though less
interesting, view of myth origin is G. S. Kirk's in *The Nature of Greek Myths:*

One of the basic truths about myths, which cannot be repeated too
often, is that they are traditional tales. Such tales develop manifold
implications and meanings according to the character, wishes and
circumstances of their tellers and audiences. Therefore they are
likely to vary in their qualities and functions. The main fault in the
modern study of myth is that it has consisted so largely of a series of
supposedly exclusive theories, each of which can be easily dis-
proved by marshalling scores of agreed instances that do not accord
with it. Yet most of these theories have seemed to illuminate *some*
myths at least; for example those of a particular form, or those
associated with a particular kind of community or culture. After
all, a theory could never begin to establish itself if there were not
certain phenomena to which it seemed more or less relevant. My
own conviction, nevertheless, is that there can be no single and

comprehensive theory of myths—except, perhaps, the theory that all such theories are necessarily wrong.[12]

Kirk's views are, alas, very reasonable, though somewhat deflating to the ardent searcher for the secret of it all. Graves has, indeed, focused initially on myths of a particular form, which he shows to have been amazingly widespread throughout Europe, northern Africa, and the Middle East. All these concern a goddess associated with moon, earth, underworld, or all three, and her relation to the God of the Waxing Year, at various times her son, lover, and sacrificial victim. These myths he classes as the "true" form, arising from ritual associated with a nature-fertility—religion. The others he puts into the euhemerist category, arising mostly from the changeover to male dominance in both social structure and religion. The scheme is probably oversimplified, like every other specialized approach to such a complex subject. But it does lend coherence to a huge jumble of evidence about the ancient world. Moreover, for Graves, it has inspired further study into biblical backgrounds, four novels (*Hercules, My Shipmate, Homer's Daughter, King Jesus, Watch the North Wind Rise*), and some excellent poetry.

4

Poetry

Robert Graves has always said he writes prose, or at least his novels, to make a living. His real calling (as in "a call to the ministry") is poetry. Although Graves is a meticulous craftsman with words and poetic rhythms, the poem always begins with inspiration, presumably provided by the Muse. The wistful J. Alfred Prufrocks of this world may mourn "I have heard the mermaids singing, each to each. I do not think that they will sing for me." But Graves, who has also heard the mermaids singing, has never relinquished them. And though Prufrock drowns when human voices wake him from his fantasy,[1] Graves's persona, like the Sacred King, endures a thousand deaths and resurrections.

> Or is it of the Virgin's silver beauty,
> All fish below the thighs?
> She in her left hand bears a leafy quince;
> When with her right she crooks a finger, smiling,
> How may the King hold back?
> Royally then he barters life for love.
>
> Her brow was creamy as the crested wave,
> Her sea-blue eyes were wild
> But nothing promised that is not performed.

"To Juan at the Winter Solstice," quoted above, is one of the best known of the poems inspired by the White Goddess mythology. The poem advises the bard that "There is one story and one story only/That will prove worth your

telling." That, of course, is the love story between the Goddess, or a woman who embodies her, and her champion.

The rules of love for the Goddess and for her lovers are
obviously different. The Goddess, after all, is eternal, and
her lovers seasonal, associated with the waxing and waning
years. To be her chosen lover brings great joy, but ultimate
destruction. Thus, the lover barters life for love. Sometimes, indeed, the Goddess is utterly promiscuous and
cruel, though usually her attention is worth all the risks.

In ancient times, certain animals were associated with
the Goddess, particularly the cat, bitch, cow, sow, owl,
dove, and crane. (Her consort had other animal forms, such
as the snake, bull, or the white roebuck.) In Graves's poem
"Cat-Goddesses" the triad expands to nine (like the powerful, Ninefold-Mountain-mother of Parnassus whom Apollo
reduced to nine little nymphs, "the Muses").[2] The poem
speaks of the "perverse habit of cat-goddesses" who, "With
coral tongues and beryl eyes like lamps/Long-legged, pacing
three by three in nines—," offer themselves indiscrimi-
nately to "tatter-eared and slinking alley-toms." They do
this simply to provoke jealousy. They promptly desert the
"gross-headed, rabbit-coloured litters" that result from such
casual unions. None of these careless offspring is the sacred
child the Goddess bears to her chosen Sacred King, symbolizing the rejuvenation of spring and the fertility of the
land.

In "Return of the Goddess," the Queen appears as a
crane, reclaiming errant frogs who had unwisely crowned a
king of their own devising. "The log they crowned as king/
Grew sodden, lurched and sank;" and the frogs, "loud with
repentance," await the Goddess's judgment day. At dawn,
the Goddess returns as a "gaunt red-legged crane" to claim
them—"Lunging your beak down like a spear/To fetch
them home again." This clever fable suggests perhaps that
men, too, erred in transferring their allegiance to a male
deity. Sooner or later, the imposter will sink, and the immortal Goddess will return.

In more human terms, in the poem "Darien," the poet
tells his son (Darien) about Darien's mother, the Muse.
"Often at moonrise I had watched her go,/And a cold shud-
der shook me/To see the curved blaze of her Cretan axe."
The Cretan axe is an emblem of the Moon Goddess; it has
both convex and concave surfaces, suggesting different
stages of the moon. She uses the Cretan axe for sacrifice;
thus, it forbodes the price of being her chosen lover. But at
last the poet confronts her and she asks:

> "Will you engender my son Darien?
> Swifter than wind, with straight and nut-brown hair,
> Tall, slender-shanked, grey-eyed, untameable;
> Never was born, nor ever will be born
> A child to equal my son Darien,
> Guardian of the hid treasures of your world."
>
> I knew then by the trembling of her hands
> For whom that flawless blade would sweep;
> My own oracular head, swung by its hair.

The poet, of course, accepts, likening Darien to a
number of superlative concepts, such as the "new green of
my hope." The poem closes: "Lifting her eyes,/She held
mine for a lost eternity./'Sweetheart', said I, 'strike now,
for Darien's sake.'" Graves's poetry is usually quite clear, but
this "strike" is deliberately ambiguous. Considering the several references to the Cretan axe, "strike" inevitably suggests
the death blow. Yet, unless the "lost eternity" represents the
consummation of their love, it is not yet the time to sacrifice
the lover. Moreover, since the poet is telling the story to
Darien, the fruit of that union, the father must have been
spared, after all. It is possible, however, that the strike refers
metaphorically to the impact of both love and death, and
also to inspiration, which is the Muse's gift to the poet. J.
M. Cohen has suggested that perhaps Darien is the emerg-
ing poetic self achieved by sacrificing the old self.[3] This
interpretation would reflect the mythology of the Sacred
King, who represents both the waning year, which must be

sacrificed, and the waxing year, which is replacing him. The ambiguous violence implied in "strike" recalls the "bright bolt" that closes the poem "The White Goddess." Spring, the poet suggests, always celebrates the Mountain Mother—

> But we are gifted, even in November
> Rawest of seasons, with so huge a sense
> Of her nakedly worn magnificence
> We forget cruelty and past betrayal,
> Heedless of where the next bright bolt may fall.

The idea of receiving the Goddess's gifts, yet escaping unscathed, is also suggested in "The Ambrosia of Dionysus and Semele," where the poet entreats Dionysus: "Little slender lad, little secret god,/Pledge her your faith in me,/ Who have ambrosia eaten and yet live." The grim fate of the Sacred King in the usual course of events is celebrated in "Dethronement," in which the dethroned is pursued and rent to pieces by the Queen's hounds—"Your hot blood an acceptable libation/Poured to Persephone, in whose domain/You shall again find peace."

Many poems that are not so obviously mythical as these nevertheless suggest some stage of the "one story only." In "Purification" the persona's wife has a nightmare of being sexually possessed by a demon. So vivid and terrifying is this seeming violation of her vows of love that she goes down and bathes in the sea, as the Great Goddess did yearly at Paphos, to renew her virginity. This poem works partly for its mythological content, but partly because of a recognition of the terrible impersonality of sexual passion, which both underlies and threatens romantic love.

The excellent short poem "The Sweet Shop around the Corner" tells of a little boy who, losing track of his mother in a crowd, grabs a strange woman's hand and drags her boisterously into a sweet shop, demanding candy. Only gradually does he realize with dread that something is wrong.

Were Mother's legs so lean, or her shoes so long,
  Or her skirt so patched, or her hair tousled and grey?
Why did she twitter in such a ghostly way?
  O, Mother, are you dead?
                              What else could a child say?

It is, of course, unnecessary for the appreciation of this
poem to realize the mythic quality of Mother turned Crone.
The poem is a model of clarity and brevity, yet achieves a
striking revelation. The child, so confident in himself and
his world of indulgent Mother and animal joys, looks suddenly upon the face of old age and death.

Only occasionally do pre-Christian deities (though
never the Goddess herself, except perhaps in "Hag-Ridden")
assume a wholly negative cast. "Good Night to the Old
Gods" celebrates the retiring of primitive gods to caves by
South Sea Island peoples. An earlier poem, "Outlaws,"
written before his involvement with the Goddess mythology, seems to associate the ancient gods with primitive subconscious impulses that may still trap the unwary.

Old gods, tamed to silence, there
  In the wet woods they lurk,
Greedy of human stuff to snare
  In nets of murk.

These diminished deities are malignant and associated with
power and lust. Starving for their sacrifices of blood and
wine, they live with "ghosts and ghouls,/And ghosts of
ghosts and last year's snow/And dead toadstools." In his
early years Graves wrote a great many conventional poems
on ghosts, monsters, and other gothic folk. He has since,
wisely, culled these from his collected poems. "Outlaws,"
however, is a much more sophisticated achievement and
deserves its retention in his 1977 collection.

When Graves was struggling with the neurosis brought
on by his war experiences, he wrote a number of poems
exploring his own fears and guilts. He thought, at that time,
that the poetic expression of these darker feelings might

achieve their exorcism, not only for himself, but also for
readers so afflicted. His terrifying dreams come alive in
"The Castle" from which there is no escape:

> Or to cry, "Nightmare, nightmare!"
> Like a corpse in the cholera pit
> Under a load of corpses;
> Or to run the head against these blind walls,
> Enter the dungeon, torment the eyes
> With apparitions chained two and two,
> And go frantic with fear—
> To die and wake up sweating by moonlight
> In the same courtyard, sleepless as before.

One of the best poems of this period is called "Down,"
in which a sick man contemplates death or madness with no
hope of recovery. He remembers with what blithe trust he
played as a child at symbolic death and resurrection—or the
plunge into the unconscious, which for the child had no
horrors.

> Once he had dropped a stone between the slabs
> That masked an ancient well, mysteriously
> Plunging his mind down with it. Hear it go
> Rattling and rocketing into secret void!
> Count slowly: one, two, three! and echoes come
> Fainter and fainter, merged in the general hum
> Of bees and flies; only a thin draught rises
> To chill the drowsy air. There he had lain
> As if unborn, until life floated back
> From the deep waters.
>   Oh to renew now
> That bliss of repossession, kindly sun
> Forfeit for ever, and the towering sky!

The subterranean rivers that allow the child mind to float
back to life and health capture the sick psyche and plunge it
irrevocably into the abyss.

>   ... whirling down to hiss below
> On the flame-axis of this terrible earth;
> Toppling upon their waterfall, O spirit...

This striking combination of associations—the mythical geography of the underworld, the well (in folk wisdom one seeks truth by looking down a well), the subconscious mind, madness and death—make this one of Graves's most original poems.

Often Graves employs more traditional gothic imagery, as in "The Castle," noted above, or "The Pier-glass." The latter uses a haunted house ambience to convey despair and guilt. The persona, a woman, compulsively returns each night to a mysterious deserted bedroom, empty except for a huge draped bed, likened to a puppet theatre for the malignant fancy, and a gloomy, cracked pier glass. Nothing lives, not even "a wainscot rat/Rasping a crust" or a "starveling spider." The woman turns to look at her reflection in the pier glass—"grey lips and long hair dishevelled,/Sleep-staring eyes." She pleads for some token of hope, somewhere "True life, natural breath; not this phantasma."

In later collections of his poems, Graves ends the poem at this point. When the poem first appeared in 1921 in the book of poems also called *The Pier-glass*, it had another twenty-five lines that suggested the motivation for the persona's despair and a dramatic shift of emotional content. Her plea for some sign of life is granted, for she discovers that bees have formed a hive between the pier glass and the wall. (Is the persona a perverted Alice trapped in a death-phantasy, while on the other side of the looking glass real life beckons where the queen bee rules?) She finds the courage, then, to reaffirm a judgment she once made about a lover who had wronged her.

> *Kill or forgive?* Still does the bed ooze blood?
> Let it drip down till every noor-plank rot!
> Yet shall I answer challenging the judgment:—
> "Kill, strike, again, again," the bees in chorus hum.

Thus, the return to emotional life, which the presence of the bees evokes, results not in repentance or peace or readjustment, but in renewed hatred and the impulse to reenact the murder. One can only speculate as to why

Graves chose to eliminate this last stanza. Perhaps he thought it a bit melodramatic, not really as good poetry as the first three stanzas. It may have touched a rage so deeply buried, however, that he later wished to retract so bold a statement of repressed violence. Without it, certainly, the poem is quite different—and in some ways, a more conventional expression of despair. If this were a later poem (after he was involved with the White Goddess), the presence of the queen bee might suggest to the persona that she was right in her ruthless destruction of the unfaithful lover. The hive serves the queen bee, and to betray her deserves death. Graves was fascinated by fatal women, though, long before he discovered the White Goddess.

Douglas Day in *Swifter Than Reason*,[4] says that Graves suffered from conflicting motivations about the degree to which his poetry should share in his mental-emotional conflicts. Graves must have known that his subjective poetry dealing with guilt, despair, neurotic fears, and unrequited love was better than the lighter poems of *Country Sentiment* (published the year before *The Pier-glass*), which suggested flight from rather than an examination of the dark areas of human experience.

Graves recognized that mental conflict sometimes enhances the sensitivity that is necessarily a part of the poetic mood. He conveys this idea in effective hyperbole in "Lost Love," which celebrates the heightened perceptions induced by unrequited love. He can see leaves grow, hear the "drinking sound of grass,/worm talk, clashing jaws of moth/Chumbling holes in cloth . . ."

According to Day, Graves "was at the same time afraid that the very emotional resolution he was trying to effect by the incorporation of his neurosis into his more serious poems might destroy his talent."[5] Just why this should be so is not explained. But Graves did become more detached and less intense in later poetry. Perhaps this was necessary for emotional reasons, but I believe that his poetry became less gripping because of that withdrawal from intensity. T. S.

Eliot, at this time, was advocating a more objective approach, but Graves informed Day that he had not read
Eliot's criticism.

Indeed, Graves meticulously avoided the admonitions
of critics and current fashions in poetry. He never joined the
sometimes frantic efforts of modern poets to throw off all
traces of nineteenth-century romanticism. "The Pier-glass"
operates very effectively in a gothic mode, just as other
poems use a more stark and modern method. "The Legs,"
for instance, is utterly original, though perhaps surrealism
suggested the half humorous, philosophical scene:

> There was this road,
> And it led down-hill,
> And round and in and out.

> And the traffic was legs,
> Legs from the knees down,
> Coming and going,
> Never pausing.

The persona recognizes "the senseless, frightening/Fate of
being legs," but is thankful that he himself stands firmly in
the grass by the roadside. Suddenly, the sense of superiority
he is obviously enjoying becomes slightly clouded with
doubt.

> My head dizzied then:
> I wondered suddenly,
> Might I too be a walker
> From the knees down?

> Gently I touched my shins.
> The doubt unchained them:
> They had run in twenty puddles
> Before I regained them.

The utter simplicity of this diction, the clarity of the
symbolic action, the recognition that any reader must feel
who strives to retain his self-possession in the midst of futile
busyness all around him, must assure this ironic poem a

long life. While it may suggest to some a neurotic division of mind and body, it is too close to any contemplative person's reality to be a symptom of abnormality.

Some of Graves's guilt-laden poems are focused on a recurring shame about physical sexuality, as compromising romantic love. The most explicit of these is "Down, Wanton, Down!" in which the persona addresses his phallus with the complaint that "Love may be blind, but Love at least/Knows what is man and what mere beast." The final two stanzas are loaded with wordplay. Here is the fourth stanza:

> Tell me, my witless, whose one boast
> Could be your staunchness at the post,
> When were you made a man of parts
> To think fine and profess the arts?

This poem seems to have particular relevance because of the popular tendency to glorify physical love as an end in itself. Graves is, in this sense, "old fashioned," refusing to accord to sheer lust any particular dignity.

In more intense examples of this sentiment, such as "The Succubus," the neurotic nightmare again reigns: "Thus will despair/In ecstasy of nightmare/Fetch you a devil-woman through the air," She comes in answer to prayer, yet never as a beautiful, lissome creature, but as a disgusting hag.

> Why with hot face,
> With paunched and uddered carcass,
> Sudden and greedily does she embrace,
> Gulping away your soul, she lies so close,
> Fathering brats on you of her own race?
> Yet is the fancy grosser than your lusts were gross?

In "Ulysses," the Greek hero is sex possessed—"never done/With woman whether gowned as wife or whore." Ulysses displays a self-contempt more indicative, surely, of the poet's mood, than of the viewpoint of myth.

> His wiles were witty and his fame far known,
> Every king's daughter sought him for her own,

> Yet he was nothing to be won or lost.
> All lands to him were Ithaca: love-tossed
> He loathed the fraud, yet would not bed alone.

Even in a later, perhaps more emotionally stable period, in "Questions in a Wood," the lover asks how he can "Vilely deliver love to death/Wrapped in a rumpled sheet?" Although a witty John Donne could dally light heartedly with the ambiguities of carnal and spiritual love, Graves seems never to have reconciled himself entirely to mundane bodies. Nor has he achieved a truly comic treatment of this complaint, such as Delmore Schwartz's delightful "The Heavy Bear Who Goes With Me."

Some of Graves's poems have both psychological and philosophical implications. "The Cool Web," for instance, suggests that language protects us from raw sense experience. Children, he claims, "are dumb to say how hot the day is" or how dreadful the approaching night or the marching soldiers. With speech we "spell away" these horrors, but this protection gradually kills us emotionally:

> There's a cool web of language winds us in,
> Retreat from too much joy or too much fear:
> We grow sea-green at last and coldly die
> In brininess and volubility.

But if we throw off language before we die and again face "the wide glare of the children's day," we shall "go mad no doubt and die that way." One suspects that the threatening, overpowering quality of naked reality was not a childhood vision for Graves, however, but one gained in early manhood during World War I. Yet, from personal experience, I suspect we tend to underestimate the horrors of childhood.

In another poem about childhood vision, "Warning to Children," an onion-like reality never reveals a core of meaning, but only repetitive layers of frivolous illusions.

> Children, if you dare to think
> Of the greatness, rareness, muchness,
> Fewness of this precious only
> Endless world in which you say

You live, you think of things like this:
Blocks of slate enclosing dappled
Red and green, enclosing tawny
Yellow nets, enclosing white
And black acres of dominoes,
Where a neat brown paper parcel
Tempts you to untie the string.

In the parcel the child will find an island, a tree, a fruit from the tree. When he strips the rind from the fruit he will find blocks of slate, and so on. He arrives, of course, at another brown paper parcel. He is warned to leave the string alone, for he will become entrapped on the island, in the fruit, with the blocks of slate around his head, trapped in the tawny yellow nets, with the same parcel still unopened in his lap. If he again dares to contemplate the greatness of his precious world, he will again untie the string. Though this poem may be read simply as a playful game, its psychological and philosophical implications of entrapment, endlessly repeated but essentially meaningless experience, are foreboding. And surely all contemplative souls, at least in their darker moods, must admit to some similar impressions of the illusory core of meaning, which always beckons, but never stands revealed.

The theme of illusion is developed in different terms in relation to the White Goddess mythology. In "The Broken Girth" an Irish knight, the Queen's lover, rides from Fairyland, on furlough. Pausing to help some Ulstermen, a broken saddle girth tumbles Oisin to the ground. "And at once, it is said,/Old age came on him with grief and frailty." St. Patrick then asks him if he will confess the Christ. In loyalty to the Fairy Queen, the knight refuses and dies.

Curse me all squint-eyed monks
Who misconstrue the passing of Finn's son:
Old age, not Fairyland, was his delusion.

Thus Christianity seems to conspire with matter to appose life and love and beauty. As Emerson said of the poet— "The dream shall be real to thee."

Yet, Graves would never rest well in Emerson's blithe romanticism, which made every fact of nature represent a truth of the spirit. In "Nature's Lineaments," nature offers little guidance to the spirit, even as lust misrepresents love. To anthropomorphize nature is to create a gross monster whose mind is only wind, whose pleasures are "excreting, poking,/Havocking and sucking,/Sleepy licking." The business of the philosopher is apparently best pursued in an utterly barren environment, isolated from the distractions of the senses, according to the poem called "The Philosopher." The scene is a bare prison with no view at all. Here is solace for a laborious mind, "Threading a logic between wall and wall/Ceiling and floor."

> Truth captured without increment of flies;
> Spinning and knotting till the cell became
> A spacious other head
> In which the emancipated reason might
> Learn in due time to walk at greater length
> And more unanswerably.

This poem seems to display neither approval nor disapproval of this mental process. In other contexts, reason has been allied to science and technology, and denigrated in favor of the heart or intuitive wisdom.

This interest in philosophy and disembodied truth probably derives from Graves's association with Laura Riding. She was in pursuit of the Truth, with a capital T, that always transcends particular truths. We are alive in the best sense, according to Riding, "by the degree to which we ourselves exist in thought, rather than in history, and place reality in meanings rather than things."[6] Riding advocated an invisible apocalypse, claiming that humanity had wallowed long enough in its sloth and immaturity. A new day dawns in which important activity is entirely mental. Graves expresses this idea in "End of Play" and possibly in "The Fallen Tower of Siloam," as well. In the former:

> We have at last ceased idling, which to regret
> Were as shallow as to ask our milk-teeth back;

As many forthwith do and on their knees
Call lugubriously upon chaste Christ.

We tell no lies now, at last cannot be
The rogues we were—so evilly linked in sense
With what we scrutinized that lion or tiger
Could leap from every copse, strike and devour us.

This obscurely Platonic view of freedom from history
and from the senses may be a pleasant personal impression.
It clashes curiously with the earlier wisdom of the Great
Mother, in which experience is bound to the cycles of nature. It seems highly unlikely that human beings as a group
are ever going to shuffle off our bondage to the senses.
Moreover, sense experience is the poet's stock in trade.

In spite of these forays into the philosophical and the
psychological, Graves is still primarily a love poet. He has
become no more philosophical with age, though some love
poems note age differences. "Two crucial generations
parted them,/Though neither chargeable as an offence—
/Nor could she dare dismiss an honest lover/For no worse
crime than mere senility." ("Two Crucial Generations.")
Age seems to make little difference in the terms of love—or
at least the mythical terms that Graves usually uses—"In
our impossible pact of only love/Which, being a man, I
honoured to excess/But you, being a woman, quietly disregarded." ("The Pact.")

This tendency to cast love almost exclusively into given
mythological patterns, which he has already explored, has
limited Graves's originality. Saying the same thing over and
over again may even destroy love itself, as he notes in "Reiteration."

Nature herself repunctuates her seasons
With the same stars, flowers, fruits—
Though love's foolish reluctance to survive
Springs always from the same mechanical fault:
The needle jumps its groove.

One welcomes the occasional new metaphor, such as

the one Graves uses in "The Oleaster." The oleaster is a tough, strong-rooted tree well suited for the rocky, inhospitable terrain of Majorca. The more delicate, but fruitful, olive trees are grafted on to the hardy oleaster roots. "The olives hang grass-green, in thankfulness/For a bitter sap and bitter New Year snows/That cleansed their bark. . . ." The poet then asks forgiveness of his beloved for saying nothing new. "I am no child of the hot sun like you,/Though in rock rooted like an oleaster." This poem has the vigor of his earlier stark description of the Welsh countryside in "Rocky Acres."

The reader sometimes yearns for a real woman with a distinct personality and particular foibles to emerge from these repeated avowals of love. When a poem like "Semi-Detached" comes along, we are shocked by the advent of real people among the abstract lovers. "Semi-Detached" is about a neighbor couple who stay together in that semidetachment that couples often come to—passion dead, appearances correct, frustration stoically endured. There is a particularity of description in "Semi-Detached" that is totally lacking in some of the abstract love lyrics, for example, from "Three Words Only":

> Sweetheart, I love you
> Here in the world's eye
> And always shall do
> With a perfect faith
> In three words only.

Poetry entirely devoid of images or particular detail creates little impact. As oft-repeated rituals of love make the needle jump its groove in "Reiteration," so "Three Words Only" offers a repetition of vacuous phrases. Moreover, Graves sometimes lapses into overuse of a particularly tedious word—no less than seven late poems employ the word "togetherness"!

All of which simply means that good poets sometimes write feeble poetry. In the past Graves has been an excellent critic of his own poetry (if not always of other people's). Had he world enough and time, which seems unlikely, some of these lesser efforts might disappear from the canon.

In his futuristic fantasy, *Watch the North Wind Rise*, the poet-protagonist brings trouble and discord into an ordered and peaceful world because "true love and wisdom spring only from calamity." Perhaps Graves has been too comfortable in his advancing years—if old age can ever be comfortable. At any rate, the calmer waters run no deeper than before.

Graves has had his share of calamity to feed on; he has produced some moving poetry out of pain. But the White Goddess mythology, which apparently helped him to surmount and codify both ecstatic and painful experiences, has been a mixed blessing. It has inspired some of his best poetry, but also prescribed limitations to growth. Though in late years he professed to increased interest in what he called the Black Goddess; a more benevolent archetype, she remains in the shadowy background, like Homer's Mother Night. She is, I suspect, the death aspect of the same mythic figure with some of her fangs removed. But she has not fired his imagination sufficiently to evoke inspired poetry equal to that created through her more savage sister.

No law of nature decrees that a person's writing ability should get better and better indefinitely—or that it should follow any other prescribed pattern, such as that suggested by the waxing and waning year. Graves, while not a truly great poet, has written some very good poems at almost every stage of his development. He should be known for his best work, and the best work occurs intermittently throughout a long and devoted career.

5

Novels Using Greek Myth

Graves based four novels specifically on his investigation of Greek myths and the goddess cults that preceded male-dominated religion. *King Jesus* and *Hercules, My Shipmate* are the most significant of these. *King Jesus* shows the lingering influence of the fertility cults; Jesus actively opposes the Goddess, yet fulfills the ancient pattern of her Sacred King. *Hercules, My Shipmate* deals with a much earlier period of history, when the interloper Zeus has been absorbed into the Goddess religion but has not yet established his superiority over her. *Watch the North Wind Rise* is a futuristic fantasy about the reestablishment of the Goddess in Crete. *Homer's Daughter*, discussed in this chapter with *Hercules, My Shipmate*, is a light novel based loosely on certain parts of the Odyssey.

In *Homer's Daughter*, Graves acts on a theory advanced by Samuel Butler in *Authoress of the Odyssey*—that the Odyssey was written by a woman, possibly self-portrayed as Nausicaa, the Sicilian princess who befriends Odysseus after he is shipwrecked on his way home from the Trojan War. This theory seems to be based partly on geography and partly on rather shaky assumptions about feminine tastes and knowledge—intimate knowledge of court life, for instance, but gross ignorance of sailing and herding economy. In *The Greek Myths*, Graves says Butler suggests "only a woman could have made Odysseus interview the famous women of the past before the famous men [in Hades] and,

in his farewell speech to the Phaeacians hope that 'they will
continue to please their wives and children' rather than the
other way about." (Odyssey xiii, 44–45) That does seem like
an unlikely sentiment in a patriarchal society, but the evidence is inconclusive.

Graves has Nausicaa living two hundred years after
Homer, thus only metaphorically Homer's daughter. At
that time professional bards were known as Sons of Homer.
Presumably the coloring she gives to the Odyssey is effected
by her personal experience, as imagined in Graves's novel.
Thus her situation in the novel of being beseiged by over a
hundred suitors, none of whom she wants, she attributes to
Penelope in the Odyssey. According to Graves in *The Greek
Myths*, at least one of the older myths had Penelope promiscuous with her suitors, while the writer of the Odyssey
made Penelope a model of chastity, endlessly avoiding a
decision about remarriage.

Nausicaa is not waiting for a husband to return, but
she is needing a champion to protect her from the suitors.
Several of them have secretly murdered her brother and
plan to overthrow her father and usurp the throne. As
though in answer to her prayers to her patroness Athene, a
handsome, destitute stranger, shipwrecked upon her shores,
becomes her suppliant. This episode replicates the encounter between Odysseus and Nausicaa in the Odyssey.
This stranger is Aethon, a foreign prince remotely related to
Nausicaa's family. She hides him with Eumaeus, the royal
family's swineherd. (In the Odyssey, Eumaeus appears as
Odysseus's loyal swineherd.)

The novel ends like the Odyssey with a grand massacre
of the rebellious suitors. Aethon, disguised as a beggar,
plays the part Odysseus has in the epic. He wields the
mighty bow of Philoctetes, a trophy of the Trojan War, long
an heirloom in the palace. Odysseus was aided by his son
Telemachus, Aethon by Nausicaa's younger brother. These
two with the swineherd and a few other loyal servants destroy the whole hall full of suitors. Nausicaa saves the resi-
dent Son of Homer from the massacre by standing in front

of him. For this service he agrees to sing the epic she proposes to write about the return of Odysseus.

Nausicaa is certainly one of the more pleasant of Graves's heroines—courageous, capable, shrewd, yet not cruel or vindictive. She does share, however, the enthusiasm of the male members of her group for blood vengeance for the murders of her brother and her uncle, who was regent in her father's absence. Aethon is a stock hero, the strong, handsome stranger who wins the hand of the princess in a trial of valor.

At the end of *The Greek Myths*, Graves says, "But though masquerading as an epic, the *Odyssey* is the first Greek novel, and therefore wholly irresponsible where myths are concerned. I have suggested the possible circumstances of its composition in another novel: *Homer's Daughter.*" By calling the Odyssey "wholly irresponsible where myths are concerned," Graves is implying that the original function of myths as religious ritual and the expression of cosmic truths has been lost by the time the Odyssey was written. They have become entertainment only. Therefore, the stories can be changed so that they are closer to the heart's desire. Odysseus escapes over and over the sacrificial death of the Sacred King, which was a part of "true" myth—that is, a narrative form expressing ancient religious ritual. And when he returns home, at last, he destroys all the young suitors and retains his possession of the queen. As Graves points out in *The Greek Myths*, Odysseus is a man (like Sisyphus) who refuses to die when he is supposed to.

Homer's Daughter, like the Odyssey is a success story wherein human intelligence, skill, and planning can remove all obstacles to happiness. Mother Night and the inexorable Wheel of Fate have receded before the sunnier Olympian gods. Nausicaa worships Athene, reborn of Father Zeus, not Artemis or Hecate or the Great Mother. Aethon serves Apollo, the god of Truth. For all this supposed rationality, however, the solution to the problem is just as bloody and violent as ever—kill all the "bad guys."

Perhaps the clue to the difference between the Iliad,

with its tragic sense of life, and the Odyssey or *Homer's Daughter* is that one is willing to categorize the suitors as bad guys and thus withdraw one's sympathy from them. The Iliad shows both Greeks and Trojans as trapped, partly by their own faults, partly by chance, partly by the force of tradition. None of the heroes is either wholly good or wholly evil. One sympathizes with all the principals, though least of all with the "romantic" lead, Paris, who would be cast as hero in a modern, B-class movie. Yet all the characters think they are doing what they have to do. *Homer's Daughter*, although seemingly the same world as that more foreboding one of the Iliad, is a more modern construct—a wish-fulfillment dream.

In a 1957 lecture now published in the book entitled *5 Pens in Hand*, Graves explained how he first became obsessed with the Triple Moon-Goddess, *alias* the Great Mother, *alias* the White Goddess. It was while he was writing *Hercules, My Shipmate*, which follows the Greek hero Jason and his famous argonauts on their voyage to regain the Golden Fleece. This novel takes place in exactly that period which fascinates Graves so much, when the worship of the Great Mother is giving way to the patriarchal supremacy of Father Zeus.

These were the days (around 1225 B.C., a generation or two before the Trojan War celebrated in Homer's Iliad) when Hera was being demoted from the absolute queen of heaven to the nagging wife of Zeus; when the terrible Artemis, goddess of the moon and the hunt, was losing ground to her brother Apollo; when Athene was reborn of Zeus's head.[1] Graves considers such mythical events as rationalizing the conquest of the prevailing goddess cults by invading patriarchal tribesmen, first the Ionians, then the Achaeans, both honoring a rain-making sky god.

But religions do not change overnight. Isolated communities held fast to the old religion of the Mother. Jason and his crew met several of these communities that still worshipped the Great Goddess as supreme. Indeed, the mission itself to return the Golden Fleece was primarily a religious quest arising from friction between native peoples and their Ionian conquerors. Nevertheless, the distinguished heroes who joined the quest, perhaps analogous to the Christian knights who went on crusades during medieval times, rather obviously were drawn by the promise of fame and adventure.

The Golden Fleece was a sacred object used to adorn the image of the sky god, Dios, worshipped in the shape of a ram by the first body of invaders into Greece, the Ionian tribe. At first, there was no particular problem about the new god, since the Ionians freely acknowledged that he was the son of the Mother Goddess. The Goddess, therefore, renamed him Zagreus, or Zeus, after the child she bore each year in the Dictean Cave and sacrificed to make the land fertile. The sacrifice was now discontinued, and Zeus was allowed the status of an adult god.

All might have been well, had the solemn Ionian men not got impatient with the orgiastic customs of the native women worshippers of the Mother Goddess, many of whom they had married. It was presumably necessary for the women to take charge of the sowing of grain and to honor the goddess by making love with many men in the plowed fields. Their usual partners in this orgiastic ritual were the somewhat wild native tribe of horse men, called centaurs, who wore the manes of horses and who worshipped the mare-headed Mother Goddess.

When a haughty king named Athamus invites Ino, the Chief Priestess of the Goddess, to marry him, he is unprepared for the general orgy which results when the barbaric centaurs join the wedding feast and entice the women to lie with them in the forest. He drives the centaurs away, killing many. To discourage their return, he removes the mare-headed image of the White Goddess from her shrine and rededicates the shrine to Zeus the Ram. The image of the Ram God was carved from an oak root and it was covered with a great ram's fleece, dyed purple and fringed with finely drawn gold wire, curled like the wool fleece. Magnificent horns of gold adorned the head.

A battle of the sexes follows this desecration of the White Goddess's shrine. The king prohibits the orgiastic ceremony of the grain fields. The men will sow the barley and pray to Zeus to fertilize it with his rain.

But the women, under Ino's inspired direction, secretly parch the seed-barley so it will not sprout. Thus, when the men sow the grain and Zeus benignly sends deluges of rain, nothing sprouts but weeds. When Athamas, in despair, consults the Oracle of Apollo at Delphi, the Pythoness who interprets the oracle says he must sacrifice his son and daughter to Zeus.

Ino hears of this proposed sacrifice and induces the children of Athanas, Phrixus and Helle, to steal the Golden Fleece and flee from Greece. They do so. Helle drowns in the Dardanian Strait, thereafter called the Hellespont, but Phrixus carries the Fleece to Colchis and presents it to King Aeetes. The king drapes it on a cypress tree in the shrine of Prometheus, guarded by a great python.

This is the situation, then, when years later Jason organizes the voyage to recover the Golden Fleece. Actually, Jason is not so valiant as myth would make him, but he had boastfully promised to perform this feat within the hearing of his uncle Pelias. Pelias is the local tyrant who wants to get rid of Jason as the rightful heir to the throne. Pelias immediately traps Jason, who hadn't really been serious, into a commitment that he cannot repudiate without losing face. Pelias figures that Jason cannot possibly return from such a venture. Not only is the king of Colchis jealous in guarding the Golden Fleece, but also the journey would take a ship through narrow, dangerous straits that are carefully guarded by enemies, the Trojans.

"Hasty-mouthed Jason" seeks advice from his wise teacher, Cheiron the centaur. Cheiron has a prophetic dream of the mare-headed Goddess, giving her consent to the voyage, provided Jason finds the body of her servant

Phrixus, who carried off the Fleece, and gives it a Greek burial. The ghost of Phrixus still hovers about his corpse in Colchis, because the Colchians do not practice cremation and burial. The Greeks thought that the spirits of unburied bodies never found rest in the underworld. The Colchians had meant no disrespect to Phrixus when he died, but their burial custom was to hang dead bodies in trees to be eaten by birds.

Thus blessed by the Mother Goddess and receiving the encouragement of several of the Olympian gods as well, including Zeus, Jason sets out in the Argo with good heart and a shipful of heroes. Many of them are kings or the sons of kings, and many were sired by the gods themselves. The one woman of his crew is the maiden Atalanta, priestess of the goddess Artemis. She is fleeter of foot than any of the men and a formidable huntress. The Argo also carries Orpheus, the sweet singer who can charm even the grim gods of the underworld with his music.[2] Orpheus has a special and very valuable function in the group. Not only can he mesmerize the crew with his chants so that they can row steadily and in perfect rhythm for many hours, he can also quiet his quarrelsome shipmates when dissent arises among them.

But the most remarkable of the argonauts is undoubtedly Hercules, who is both a marvelous asset and a danger to his shipmates. He is a huge, incredibly strong man, seven feet tall, and dangerous primarily because he does not know his own strength. His companions are always in a somewhat precarious situation, especially if there is drinking going on. A jovial pat on the back or shove from Hercules in his cups could kill a man, and a fit of temper could decimate a roomful. He is "between labors," at the moment, and glad to elude the agent of his enslavement, who could show up at any moment to order him to another impossible task. The labors of Hercules were penance arranged by the gods to expiate the guilt Hercules incurred when he had accidentally killed his own children. To be sure, Hercules is always very remorseful when he inadvertently kills his friends, but this hardly benefits the victims.

Hercules has with him his adopted son, Hylas, whom he loves dearly. Hercules has raised the boy since he had accidentally made him an orphan by killing his father. Hylas is not unappreciative of the exaggerated affection of his protector, but like any adolescent boy chafes occasionally in his role of dependent child, especially to a man whose physical prowess he can never hope to match.

The argonauts have many an adventure in the course of their voyage, most of them celebrated in myth. Many have a direct bearing on the religious issues of the time. They have a short orgiastic holiday on the island of Lemnos, for instance, inhabited entirely by women. The Lemnian women had murdered all their men, because the men had tried to replace the worship of the Triple Goddess with the Olympian gods, and had sought to dominate the women who ruled clan life. The men, meeting resistance from Lemnian women, had raided Thrace and brought back subservient women as wives. During the time of festival, when the men were all drunk, the Lemnian women maddened themselves by chewing ivy leaves and dancing naked in the moonlight. Then they swooped down upon the settlement, and killed both the men and their Thracian women. They also destroyed all their men-children, keeping only females.

By the time the argonauts touch their shores, however, the women are yearning for the company of men, both for sheer lust and for the pleasures of motherhood. So this fine group of Greek heroes have come at a propitious time, just when the Lemnians have decided they must raise up a new generation of devout men in the service of the Mother Goddess. Hercules, who does all things to excess, obliges them mightily by impregnating no less than fifty women, while Jason dallies more moderately with Queen Hypsipyle. The crew would probably have lingered there for months if Orpheus hadn't called them back to their task after three days with his irresistible music.

Hylas, though strictly confined to the ship during the orgy of Lemnos, sees the daughter of Queen Hypsipyle and falls in love with her. He promises to escape at the first opportunity and return to her at Lemnos. Hylas makes good his promise before they get to Colchis, at least the part of eluding his foster father. When his absence is discovered, Hercules goes dashing off into the wilderness in search of his beloved protégé. Jason soon sails off without Hercules, a desertion later revenged by Hercules upon the two argonauts who advised Jason to leave. Actually, Jason is glad enough to abandon Hercules, for all exploits shine feebly in the light of his gargantuan capabilities.

The argonauts manage to slip through the dangerous Trojan narrows by sailing at night with a soot-blackened sail. After many more adventures, they arrive at their destination at Colchis, where they are greeted with politeness, if not warmth. There Jason displays his own peculiar asset, in which he excels all of his shipmates. He is extraordinarily handsome and has no trouble in making Medea, the princess, fall madly in love with him. Luckily, Medea is the chief priestess of the shrine of Prometheus. She feeds the huge python that guards the Golden Fleece, so only she can approach it safely and administer the immobilizing drug that allows Jason to take the fleece.

The argonauts have several narrow escapes from the Colchian fleet that pursues them after the theft, but at last they are free. In order to affect that escape, Jason ambushes and murders Medea's brother, and hacks him to pieces. As the only heir now to the Colchian throne (Atalanta having already killed King Aeetes), Medea cooperates by ordering that her brother's body be gathered up piece by piece for honorable burial by his soldiers. The argonauts meanwhile escape with Medea and the Golden Fleece, while the Colchian soldiers look for the scattered remains of their former leader.

The blood spilled on this occasion requires a side trip to another high priestess of the goddess, Circe. The sor-

ceress Circe is perhaps better known for having detained
Odysseus on his journey home from Troy and having
turned his men into swine. She is the only person powerful
enough to purify the blood guilt of such murderers.

Thus Zeus regains his Golden Fleece, the argonauts
get lasting fame and glory, and Jason gets the beautiful
princess. But myth is too close to the reality of human life
for everybody to live happily ever after. The Greeks, more
than most, knew that success is a seasonal affair and the
wheel of fortune always brings down the hero.

The last of the novel traces the various fates of the
argonauts, some of them pleasant, but many tragic. As a
later tragedian warned, call no man fortunate who is not
dead. Not that death itself is fortunate, but that life is always
uncertain and usually changes for the worst. Hylas never
makes it back to Lemnos, but dies enroute. Hercules dies in
agony of poison administered by his wife, who thought she
was giving him a love potion. Jason, though he spends some
years happily married to Medea, eventually divorces her to
marry someone who offers him political advantages. The
outraged Medea, as great in hate as in love, poisons her rival
and her rival's father, kills her children by Jason, and escapes, leaving Jason without heirs. This is the part of the
story immortalized in the play *Medea* by Euripides. Jason
dies finally as he sits sadly under the prow of the Argo,
which had been dedicated to Poseidon, the sea god. The
Argo has fallen into disrepair and suddenly the whole prow
falls away, killing Jason instantly.

Myths and legends seldom indulge in complicated
characterizations. Characters are distinguished by their
function in the plot. Yet the Greeks were conscious very
early of the incongruities between stereotyped heroes and
real people. They were among the first to introduce irony
and parody into literature.

Graves has sought to evoke both the simple heroic
consciousness and the comic parody. The argonauts, with
the exception, perhaps, of Jason and Hercules, are hardly

distinguishable one from another. Orpheus and Atalanta are different only because of their well-known specialized abilities. One argonaut is an expert on bees and another understands the language of birds. But there is no analysis of anybody's secret consciousness, nor even any discernible differences in speech.

The character of Jason is quite clear and consistent— and true to the ironic characterization provided by Euripides in *Medea*. He is a handsome, somewhat rash, usually selfish young man, conscious of his attractiveness to women. He is ill matched to one so intense and passionate as Medea.

Hercules is a parody of the heroic adventurer. His famous twelve labors, such as cleaning the Augean stables in a hurry by deflecting a river, are very like some of the tall tales of Paul Bunyan. His sexual potency is a parody of the great lover. His mindless sentimentality over Hylas is a parody of parental nurture. His physical prowess, which in moderation is the ideal of a warrior people, becomes gross and absurd. He is the living illustration of the Greek philosopher's observation that vice can be simply the excess of virtue.

But primitive storytellers are always adept at comical exaggeration. Graves writes in the Historical Appendix at the end of the book:

The sexual vigor of Hercules, like his gluttony, was always comic to the Greeks, and his tremendous night of copulation with the fifty daughters of Peneus may be compared with the feats of such bawdy folk-heroes as the French Marius, the English Stone-Cracker John, the American Paul Bunyan, or the Trobriander, mentioned in Malinowski's *Sexual Life of Savages*, whose phallus was so long it used to go creeping about the village after dark seducing unwary village girls.

Graves's tone and point of view in this novel has been chosen very carefully and rigorously maintained. He discusses this problem in the Historical Appendix, where he explains:

Here it would have been unwise to tell the story as from the thirteenth century B.C.: this would have meant writing the story in poetic pictographs. To tell it as from the present day would not only have meant recording conversation in an unsuitably modern style, but would have prevented me from believing wholeheartedly in the story. The only solution was to take up my position in an age which still believed, but which had achieved the required critical detachment and a plain but dignified prose style.

Where Graves writes "today" and "to this day," it means not later than 146 B.C., when Roman soldiers sacked Corinth. According to an epigram by Martial, Graves says, pieces of the Argo were brought back to Rome as souvenirs.

This observation illustrates the sustained implication that the journey of the argonauts was probably historical. It was, at least, widely believed and recorded by many ancient writers. Indeed, as Graves interprets the tale, it is possible, if not plausible in every detail. The people and events preserve the legendary view of heroes somewhat larger than life; yet, everything is rooted in the natural, not the supernatural.

In this meticulous avoidance of the supernatural, Graves illustrates how some of the more fanciful details of ancient myths and legends may have had a purely natural origin. The centaurs, for instance, were not half men, half horse, as they are pictured, but members of a fraternity that considered the horse their totem animal and adorned themselves with horse's manes. Jason belonged to the leopard fraternity and wore a leopard skin. Each of the heroes had his sacred animal; so also did the gods.

Similarly, the dragon said to guard the Golden Fleece was only a huge python, but, after all, a python is sufficiently terrifying to keep most mortals at a distance, even if it doesn't breathe fire. And Medea, though she was said to be a witch, was simply wise in the herbs and natural drugs that have always been used by shamans.

The lineage of the demigods—that is, those persons who claim one of the gods as a parent—is inconspicuously revealed in a way quite plausible anthropologically. Since many ancient cults celebrated the reproductive powers of nature, temples sometimes had holy prostitutes, whose children were presumably engendered by the deity they served. Or a woman's first child might be fathered by a priest in the temple, who served as a stand-in for his god. Christians have been embarrassed by the early associations between sexuality and religion and have conveniently forgotten what "the first child belonging to the church" may once have implied. Graves does not interrupt his narrative to explain these matters, but conveys them quite subtly, in keeping with a narrator who accepts such relationships as common knowledge.

The gods speak to men in dreams or in drug-induced hallucinations. In other words, they issue from the human imagination, which by no means makes them less potent. When the gods change, it is because men change in their perception of reality. The mythical gods are real and imminent in a way that the remote and theoretical god of a much later time can never be. They are as close as love and hate and fear and death to people who live in daily contact with these elemental experiences. They are powerful and unpredictable like the forces of nature they represent. "The concept of the supernatural is a disease of religion," Graves wrote in 5 Pens in Hand. "True religion is of natural origin and linked practically with the seasons, though it implies occasional states of abnormal ecstasy which can be celebrated only in the language of myth."

In adopting this attitude toward the gods, Graves maintains a tone comparable, in some ways, to Homer's Iliad. Every case of seeming supernaturalism in the Iliad could also be removed without changing the story line, for everything that happens could as well be attributed to natural causes.

Moreover, Homer's view of the gods follows logically in the direction of change that Graves illuminates. When Homer wrote, even the Trojan War was long gone, an historical legend. The Great Mother cult, still strong in the days of the argonauts, had receded into the primitive past.

The Zeus of the Iliad is more powerful than all the other Olympian gods put together. Aphrodite, goddess of love and beauty, who once had powerful cults of her own, has very little dignity left; Hera is a shrew, and Athene, though formidable, is an extension of Father Zeus. The moon goddess, Artemis, still throws her weight around in a disturbing way, but her influence is marginal. The Great Mother has receded into the background. Only occasionally do the gods speak of the mysterious Mother Night, of whom even Zeus stands in awe. Nevertheless, the Great Mother still rules remotely as Fate, the Goddess beyond all gods, leaving the petty competition for men's adoration to her squabbling children.

6

Graves
and the Mythological Future

Watch the North Wind Rise (published in England as *Seven Days in New Crete*) is a utopian fantasy that uses certain conventions of science fiction and literary utopias, combined with mythical themes. A witch's magic, rather than a pseudoscientific time machine, provides the time travel. The protagonist, Edward Venn Thomas, is evoked by the witch Sally to an indefinitely distant future when the Bronze and Early Iron Ages have been purposely reestablished as the most successful pattern for peaceful human existence. The colony of New Crete, created on pre-Christian and prepatriarchal models by an Anthropological Society, has a strictly limited technology, a caste system based on native capacity and temperament (not intelligence or education), and an orderliness based on custom backed by religion, rather than on a body of written laws.

The world had amply proved, by this time, that rationality alone, no matter how sophisticated or scientific it might become, could never create the Golden Age. The last widespread philosophy on a world scale had been Logicalism, supported by international science. It rejected both religion and nationalism. But it resulted in a pervasive sense of futility, for it could offer no more compelling a motivation for action than efficiency. Though war was no longer possible with the demise of nationalism, poetry and the arts languished in a society that valued only logical, utilitarian thinking. Scientists devoted themselves to the fur-

ther proliferation of knowledge, none of which resulted in
any increased human happiness.

The inhabitants of New Crete, therefore, evolve a
new-old religion as a basis for all social customs, choosing
an agricultural-matriarchal model akin to the religion of
pre-Christian Europe. The Queen of Heaven is Mari, a
deity based on that familiar moon-earth-underworld trinity
known in ancient times as Semele-Demeter-Persephone, or
Artemis-Aphrodite-Hecate, and by many other names.
Mari may appear as Numaë the Maiden or Ana the Mother
or Crone. Earthly queens represent Mari in each kingdom
of New Crete. Each queen keeps a Sacred King who rules
for seven years, then is sacrificed to keep the land fertile,
and replaced by another consort. Religious observances are
attuned to agricultural festivals and handicraft mysteries.

Local myths support the notion of a male trinity only
in negative terms. Popular folktales tell of the rebellion of
the Drones who repudiated the Queen Bee (their Goddess),
led by Machna the god of Science, Dobeis the god of
Money, and Pill the god of Theft.

The five estates, each of which performs a valuable
function in New Crete society, are captains, recorders,
commons, servants, and magicians. Neither captains nor
magicians actually rule, though they have limited functions
designed to keep the society on the path of custom. Children are assigned caste from early evidence of temperamen-
tal affinity to one caste or another. There are ways to change
one's caste in the case of late-blooming capabilities hitherto
unrecognized. Presumably, as in Plato's *Republic*, everyone
is contented with his caste because he is among those of like
interests and life style. But this is not, as Plato would have
it, indicated by the ability to master abstract thinking and
advance in formal studies.

As a matter of fact, this is not a bookish society, since
paper and printing are both banned. A recorder can keep
records, and poets (generally of the magician class) can write
poems, temporarily, on clay tablets. Only when a poem is

judged by one's peers as having lasting value may it be engraved on silver or gold plates, to be preserved for posterity. The number of these is strictly limited. Thus, literature and written knowledge is deliberately cut to the very bone. It is at last possible to be a true "Renaissance man," having read all available learning, and only the very best. But persons of the common and servant castes are taught orally and need not read. (So much for the familiar agonies of universal education, and the exploitation of word-pollution resulting from unrestrained printing. Even those of us who make our living with books have an ironic sympathy for such restrictions.)

One of the more entertaining institutions of New Crete is the Nonsense House, absolutely taboo to all but the elders. No one knows what goes on there, but Edward dares to enter because he has a protective amulet from the Goddess herself. The elders in the Nonsense House can do anything they please there, even in gross violation of custom. They can read books, have brawls or orgies, or otherwise sow their wild oats, so long as they resume the accustomed decorum when they venture out into society. Newcomers often get a cruel hazing when they first enter—even from former lovers. Does not all love include some hate?

"War" is declared during Edward's visit, due to a disagreement between members of neighboring villages. War is a rough game somewhat similar to an Old English game of Shrovetide football. The men are all well greased and almost naked, armed only with a light quarterstaff padded on one end. The game is to carry a war token to a particular spot in the rival village square. Injuries are few; if a death occurs accidentally, the war stops immediately. At the end of the day both villages join in a peace banquet.

The society bans money altogether, and want is virtually unknown. The countryside is exceedingly fertile. Since the earth is sacred to the Mother, all wastes are carefully returned to her in the best organic gardening style. There is a marketplace for each community where one

brings gifts, in Mari's name, of any surplus goods or handi-
crafts, and selects freely whatever one needs in return. It is
religiously unthinkable to hoard more food than one can eat
or more clothes than one can wear. And to work with love is
both a joy and an act of piety.

Only gradually does Edward understand why he, a
relative barbarian, is brought back to this ordered society. As
a poet, he is already a devoted follower of the Muse, his
version of their Goddess. His presence brings disorder again
into a society so lacking in competition and tension that
intensity had been all but lost. Men, though properly respectful and obedient to superior female wisdom, have become altogether too meek and mild. Edward notices this
diminished intensity particularly in the feeble poetry, written by the male magicians, whose function is to call the
Goddess to witness and inspire some magical action.

The novel ends when a crowd of inhabitants finally
turns on Edward for having poisoned their community. He
then becomes the magician, drawing a magic circle around
himself and a girl child, and prophesies in the name of the
Blessed Goddess. He cries out in his invocation: "She
summoned me from the past, a seed of trouble to endow
you with a harvest of trouble, since true love and wisdom
spring only from calamity. . . ." He calls upon the North
Wind to blow away security. "And this is the sign
prophesied from her whirlwind, and its vortex will be the
circle in which this stormchild and I now stand. You will be
caught in that baleful gust, you will gasp and sicken, and
carry the infection to every town and village in this kingdom; migrant birds and insects will carry it farther, to all the
kingdoms of New Crete; and the symptoms of the infection
will be an itching palm, narrowed eyes and a forked tongue."

Then he asks the girl, whom he loves, to cling tightly
to his hair. He calls upon the Goddess to return him to his
own time, which she does. Only a moment of his own time
has elapsed. It is night and he lies down beside his drowsy
wife to impregnate her with the daughter he has always
wanted.

Watch the North Wind Rise, though easily dismissed as a light novel written for a mass audience, is nevertheless something of a *tour de force*. Though it hasn't the sober didactic message of Edward Bellamy's *Looking Backwards* or B. F. Skinner's dull *Walden Two*, it makes some of the familiar judgments upon our highly commercialized, militaristic society. But it also satirizes literary utopias themselves, with their often heavy-handed, mechanistic rearrangements of life styles and technology.

With his customary antimodern perversity, Graves vehemently rejects the notion that rationality and scientific technology can ever achieve the envisioned goals of "progress." If you want a truly peaceful, ordered society, he seems to say, you must discard practically everything this society holds most dear: not just money and accumulative wealth, but technology itself, which has always invited destructive military uses. Even the printing press must go, for words are now used more for deception than for illumination.

Moreover, neither Christianity with its masculine deity, so easily subverted to economic or military interests, nor the materialism that has largely replaced Christianity, can bring back sanctity to human life or to a deliberately demythologized nature. A successful utopia would have to cast aside not only industrialization, but also the whole notion of male supremacy either on earth or in heaven.

The local war, though fought with great enjoyment for utterly frivolous reasons, reflects Graves's nostalgia for stylized conflict. In the lead essay of *But It Still Goes On*, a follow-up to his autobiography, Graves contrasts modern mechanized conflict with the function of war in other, presumably more primitive, societies. In spite of his shattering experience in the trenches, he does not repudiate war *per se*, but only modern war. "State-organized frightfulness in war," he says, "is an innovation in Europe." Most matters are more sensibly handled by arbitration; everyone knows that modern wars are disastrous whether you win or lose. But some issues are better settled in physical conflict, so long as it is contained within prescribed limits.

Fighting in man is as ineradicable an instinct as love, with which
of course it has much in common; the chief common quality
being romanticism, without which love would be mere sexual
convenience and fighting either necessary slaughter or unavoid-
able self-defence. To most men the idea of submitting questions of
honour to arbitration is as distasteful as would be that of having
their love-affairs regulated by a committee of eugenic experts.

Though Graves is talking here about personal honor,
he admits later in the discussion that this sentiment attaches
itself to the feeling of prestige for one's nation or group.
(Graves has revealed this tendency himself in his active
interest in the history and venerable reputation of the Royal
Welsh Fusiliers, his World War I battalion.) It is mechani-
zation that has ruined warfare, depriving it of its only real
service to human affairs. The Japanese, Chinese, Maoris,
American Indians, and even medieval knights have, in the
past, stylized and contained the destructiveness of war. He
therefore proposes some regulations for the conduct of honorable war, which he admits is a concession to a somewhat
childish rivalry among men. Then he adds:

Reformed war, of some such sort as this, childish though it may
seem, is the only logical substitute for the modern war in which
nobody now believes. Nationalism is a primitive, or, if you will, a
childish national sentiment. It is better to be admittedly childish
and play the game of national honour in as romantic and innocuous a way as honour allows, than to pretend to be sophisticated and
be ready to commit moral, mental and economical suicide by
playing the same game with the most universally destructive
weapons that come to hand. I suggest that the first reformed war
should be fought on Swedish territory—admirably suited to
manoeuvre—between Italy and France, those two most glory-
loving powers. The Nobel Peace Prize Committee could under-
take the task of drawing up an experimental code.

This not altogether serious proposal is dramatized in
even more playful terms in the war episode in New Crete.
The conflict is caused by differences over the question of
whether a rebellious youngster, who ran away to the next
village, should have to eat damson jam every night for sup-

per. Men never grow up; and women, though more sensible, will go along with the fun and bestow their favors on the valiant. After the battle, as Edward walks through the dark forest, he almost stumbles over one of the captains of the recent fray enjoying the attentions of an appreciative village lass.

Besides its satirical observations about social institutions, this novel is about the mystery of women as viewed by men or, put more bluntly, man's fascination and fear of female sexuality. That element is by no means subconscious or hidden; much of the novel concerns Edward's struggle to achieve the "right" attitude towards various women in both his own and this future world.

In his own time, Edward is happily married and has three sons. He had once had a stormy love-hate affair, however, with a fascinating but unscrupulous woman named Erika. Edward meets Erika unexpectedly in New Crete, though no one else catches a glimpse of her. He finally realizes that she is the Goddess herself who chooses this form to communicate with him.[1]

Two other women of New Crete pull Edward's emotions in opposite directions. They are part of a living group of two women and three men, all of the magician estate, who welcome him to their house. The beautiful witch Sally covets his love, but induces a somewhat fascinated revulsion. He is immediately drawn to the younger woman, Sapphire, however. They are instantly paired by the other magicians, who intuitively perceive his true inclinations. Edward, however, is both pleased and confused, for he is not sure whether he is supposed to become her lover or what the moral implications of such a relationship might be. Actually, this somewhat comic dilemma never becomes an issue. Though they sleep together, he always falls asleep instantly as soon as he rests his head on her arm.

As a matter of fact, the magician caste has perfected a spiritualized noncarnal love, which they still consider sexual in nature. It involves lying side by side or foot to foot without other bodily involvement. One suspects that Graves

has in mind the ethereal communion described by John
Donne in "The Extasie":

> As 'twixt two equall Armies, Fate
>   Suspends uncertaine victorie,
> Our soules, (which to advance their state,
>   Were gone out,) hung 'twixt her, and mee.
>
> And whil'st our soules negotiate there,
>   Wee like sepulchrall statues lay;
> All day, the same our postures were,
>   And wee said nothing, all the day.
>
> If any, so by love refin'd,
>   That he soules language understood,
> And by good love were growen all minde,
>   Within convenient distance stood,
>
> He (though he knew not which soule spake,
>   Because both meant, both spake the same)
> Might thence a new concoction take,
>   And part farre purer then he came.

When a woman decides with whom she wishes to have
children, she gives him the "rights of fatherhood" and they
remain married thereafter. There is another curious feature
of this mating arrangement that Edward discovers in rather
grisly circumstances. If a couple have sexual intercourse on
the grave of someone who has just died, the soul of the dead
person will be reborn as the fruit of that union.

It is with this in mind, that Sally causes Figbread, one
of her housemates who loved her dearly, to be trampled to
death by his horse. Sally then kills the horse and mes-
merizes Edward so that he buries them in the forest. Then
she spreads her cloak upon Figbread's grave and tries to
seduce Edward. He is fascinated, but nevertheless pro-
foundly shocked by such an offer. When she starts a magic
incantation against him, he foils her plot by invoking the
protection of the Goddess.

In even more strange and, to Edward, terrifying de-
velopments, Sapphire ritually kills Sally, condemns herself

to ritual death, and is reborn as a member of the commons, while Edward is away watching the war. He eventually finds Sapphire again among the commons where she is undergoing an accelerated childhood quite oblivious to her former life as a witch. It is this child, whom he names Stormbird, who accompanies him home in spirit, clinging to his hair, presumably to be born again as his daughter.

As anyone even remotely acquainted with Freud can plainly see, this story deals imaginatively with some of the more murky sexual impulses of the human psyche. The sinister, magical potency of Sally's mature sexuality, the protagonist's vaguely incestuous attraction to the maiden, the bewildering metamorphoses of the Goddess as both good and evil, the sadomasochistic implications of male sacrificed to woman's purposes, the killing of the siren by the virgin. . . . A morbid, gothic novel could deal with these issues quite offensively, or at least melodramatically, but Graves's touch is light and graceful.

Yet, in spite of the light tone, the dread of female sexuality occurs over and over in the uneasy transformations of virgin, siren, mother. When Edward lies down, he assumes a child's position. Sapphire draws him to her breast but mercifully blots out consciousness, which protects him from carnal thoughts. Sally kills (castrates?) her sexual partner, and implicates Edward in the killing (Oedipal anxiety?). He shudders with horror and desire before Sally's passion, calling upon the Goddess-mother to protect him. He does not know that mother, virgin, and siren are ultimately the same. He is naïvely off guard when his wife appears, but soon learns that wife may be indistinguishable from siren. In Sapphire's absence, Sally has visited his bed in the likeness of his wife and had her way with him after all. Like Ulysses, he "loathed the fraud."

> To the much-tossed Ulysses, never done
> With woman whether gowned as wife or whore,
> Penelope and Circe seemed as one; . . .

This fall from chastity spells disaster. The virgin with-
draws from his bed and destroys her rival. Ultimately Edward reaffirms his devotion to the mother (as the Goddess)
and the virgin, who has regressed further into protective
childhood. He returns to his own time with the promise of
the purely filial devotion of a daughter. Perhaps he has won
through to a more spiritual love of the Goddess.

To change the psychological orientation, a Jungian
might say that Graves is obsessed with his anima, that
archetypal figure who presumably represents the repressed
feminine element in every man. According to Jung, the
anima in man, or the corresponding male animus in a
woman's psyche, acts as the link between the conscious and
the unconscious mind. It is thus vital to creativity, particularly to poets, who seek to express emotional experience.
Graves would probably reject this concept, judging from
wholly negative assessments he has made of Jung. Graves
prefers to account for his myth structure anthropologically.
Yet, the historical existence of a goddess cult in the ancient
world by no means explains its importance to Graves himself in imaginative creativity. His involvement with the
White Goddess mythology as an endless source of poetic
inspiration seems remarkably appropriate for Jungian explanation. Yet Jung's ideas are impossible to validate in any
objective sense. We have not yet fathomed the mystery of
creative imagination.

Feminists might protest that Graves, for all his deifica-
tion of the female, is (like Jung, perhaps) thoroughly sexist
in his thinking. Graves exaggerates the conventional view
that women are complementary, or perhaps altogether
alien, to men in temperament and capacity: that they are
less rational but more intuitive; closer to nature, yet, like
nature, amoral; less sentimental, yet more passionate. It
certainly is not the insipid Victorian stereotype of woman as
weak and tenderhearted, but it does reinforce that older,
romantic image of the fatal woman, *La belle dame sans
merci*. But to protest that Graves misrepresents woman is

probably quite irrelevant. What the novel demonstrates is not the nature of woman, but the structure of myth that dominates the poet's thinking.

Martin Seymour-Smith, in his study, *Robert Graves*, writes:

The action of . . . a 'futuristic' novel like *Seven Days in New Crete* is trivial and fantastic in itself, and throws no light at all on the complexities of human behavior. This is really because Graves is not interested in ordinary human behavior for its own sake, but only in human behavior when it conforms to, or illustrates, some mythological or pre-determined pattern.[2]

This analysis of Graves's interest is probably accurate, though the judgment of its triviality might be argued. The myth-making propensity of the human mind is in itself an important part of human behavior. Graves is not suggesting that objective reality is ever going to be like his fantastic New Crete. He does suggest, comically in this novel, seriously in *The White Goddess*, that people, or at least poets, need a mythological frame of reference. In so far as the myth may throw light on men's imaginative and emotional nature, it reveals significant human behavior.

It would be impertinent to complain that the novel is not a successful utopia, if one means by that a sourcebook for ideas to restructure society. No group of dissidents is likely to form a new commune using this novel as a guide, as persons have done with *Walden Two*. It is closer to poetry in spirit than to a sociological argument. The plot itself, the destruction of a new Eden, suggests that utopia is impossible anyway. Here, Graves seems to suggest, is the best of all possible worlds, but even it is not good enough. It can be known only imaginatively as an inspiring dream to intensify the quality of love in the painful present. Graves has never been devoted to saving the world. He has been concerned, by emotional necessity, with preserving his integrity—and, by extension, perhaps, the poetic imagination—from the depredations of a materialistic society.

7

Hebrew Mythology

This chapter concerns the alpha and the omega of Graves's writing about the Hebrew tradition. *My Head! My Head!* (1925), a short novel about Elisha and Moses, was Graves's first attempt at converting ancient history or myth into fiction. It was begun, as most of Graves's subsequent novels were, because the original accounts were somewhat mysterious, leaving much unsaid about what really happened and why. His last work on Hebrew tradition, written in collaboration with the prominent Hebrew scholar, Raphael Patai, is *Hebrew Myths: The Book of Genesis* (1963).

Actually, *Hebrew Myths* is neither as speculative or original, perhaps, as that first novel. Most people are probably less familiar with the Hebrew myths that developed around Old Testament events and characters than they are with Greek myth. They have been collected before, however, in substantially the same form as that presented by Graves and Patai. Joseph Gaer, for instance, recounts not only the Genesis myths but also those connected with later books of the Old Testament in *The Lore of the Old Testament*. [1]

In the early part of the twentieth century, Louis Ginsburg systematically collected Jewish legend and folklore in seven volumes entitled *The Legends of the Jews*. He used mainly the Talmudic-Midrashic literature that extends from the second to the fourteenth century. [2] This is the primary scholarly work on the subject. As Moses Hadas pointed out, however, Graves and Patai used some new material from the Ancient Near East, which was not yet known when Ginsburg was writing.[3]

There is one important difference between either the Ginsburg or the Gaer collections and Graves-Patai's, however: the former simply offer the stories; the latter follows each story with sources and commentaries. In fact, *Hebrew Myths* is patterned after Graves's *The Greek Myths*. The commentaries try to distinguish folk tale origin from historical origin, explain the influx of foreign elements into Hebrew contexts, note analogies between mythical heroes, and so on, just as Graves had done with the Greek myths. Some of the stories are biblical, some derive from apocryphal works, some from that great bulk of rabbinical commentaries on the Old Testament.

Hebrew myths are more nationalistic and more narrowly focused on a specialized religious function than the Greek myths are. This is partly because the Hebrews developed a strict ethical monotheism while others were still recognizing a variety of gods and goddesses, each with its own traditional tales. Moreover, prebiblical Hebrew sacred documents have been purposely suppressed or lost. Several are mentioned in the Bible. Later Hebrews sought to purify their sacred writings of pagan vestiges, though some still remain.

The definition Graves and Patai provide for myth is this: "Myths are dramatic stories that form a sacred charter either authorizing the continuance of ancient institutions, customs, rites and beliefs in the area where they are current, or approving alterations." They admit that many people believe biblical characters are historical, rather than mythical. Yet, perhaps this is a difficulty simply because these stories, at least the biblical ones, unlike most considered mythical, have many contemporary believers. The term mythical does not really deal with the issue of literal truth.

The authors explain some myths in historical terms, though more often in connection with actions of whole tribes or dynasties of kings, rather than specific persons. Migrations, subjugation to an enemy, or conquering of a new land are of sufficient group importance to warrant the support of traditional tales. The Old Testament is, perhaps more than almost any document in the world, a "sacred charter." It records the making and breaking of sacred covenants between Jehovah and his chosen people.[4]

The first covenant, of course, was with Adam and Eve in the Garden of Eden. The breaking of that bond, when the first couple ate the fruit of the forbidden Tree of the Knowledge of Good and Evil, brought sin and death into the world. Because of it, God cursed woman with painful childbirth, man with continual labor for food, and both with inevitable death.

The myth of Paradise and the Fall of Man has a whole cluster of fascinating elaborations and analogous situations in other mythologies. Graves and Patai compare the story to the Gilgamesh Epic wherein the noble savage Enkidu, who lives in perfect harmony with wild beasts, is initiated into the mysteries of love by the priestess of Aruru. After that, though Enkidu is wise as the gods, the wild creatures shun him, and he goes to live with the human race. The title of the love-goddess Aruru, or Ishtar, was "the Mother of All Living," the same title Adam gives to Eve.

Enkidu becomes wise through sexual initiation. Some writers have pointed out that "knowledge" in the Bible often means sexual intercourse, as in "he knew his wife and she conceived." Graves and Patai do not particularly pursue this lead, but consider some other novel possibilities for the knowledge of good and evil. The forbidden fruit that induces wisdom might have something to do with hallucinogenetic mushrooms, common throughout Europe and Asia. They were introduced into sacred cakes eaten at both Greek and Arabian Mysteries.

Ambrosia eaters often enjoy a sense of perfect wisdom, resulting from a close co-ordination of their mental powers. Since 'knowledge of good and evil,' in Hebrew, means 'knowledge of all things, both good and evil,' and does not refer to the gift of moral choice, the 'Tree of Life' may have once been the host-tree of a particular hallucinogenetic mushroom. For example, the birch is host to the *amanita muscaria* sacramentally eaten in certain Palaeo-Siberian and Mongol tribes.

This touch is undoubtedly due to Graves, who knew R. Gordon Wasson, an American banker, and his Russian-born wife Valentina, who, Graves says, first called attention to the close association between primitive religion and mushrooms.[5]

Eve's creation from Adam's rib and her tempting of Adam to eat the forbidden fruit exhibit that common tendency in myth to demote women from the spiritual supremacy that Graves claims they once held.

All gardens of delight are originally ruled by goddesses; at the change from matriarchy to patriarchy, male gods usurp them. A serpent is almost always present. Thus, in Greek myth, the Garden of the Hesperides, whose apple-trees bore golden fruit, was guarded by the Serpent Ladon, and had been Hera's demesne before she married Zeus, though her enemy Heracles eventually destroyed Ladon with Zeus's approval. The jewelled Sumerian paradise to which Gilgamesh went, was owned by Siduri, Goddess of Wisdom, who had made the Sungod Shamash its guardian; in later versions of the epic, Shamash has degraded Siduri to a mere 'ale-wife' serving at a near-by tavern.

For the benefit of those who know only the Bible stories repeated piously in Sunday school, or perhaps not even those, the Hebrew myths are not dull. Probably many Christians have never heard of the scandalous Lilith, Adam's first wife. Perhaps she is better known now than formerly, since women liberationists resurrected the story to show they hardly invented an issue. God created man and woman at the same time, according to one of the two biblical versions of their creation. Readers presume this woman was Eve, later said to have been created after Adam from one of his ribs. This first woman, scholars tell us, was

Lilith, whose name has since been excised from the biblical account. Lilith expected equality with Adam and became annoyed when he insisted that she lie beneath him in lovemaking. "It is characteristic of civilizations where women are treated as chattels that they must adopt the recumbent posture during intercourse. That Greek witches who worshipped Hecate favored the superior posture we know from Apuleius; and it occurs in early Sumerian representations of the sexual acts. . . ." Lilith deserted Adam and coupled with the devil instead, bearing to him countless demons (called Lilim). Lilith, jealous of Eve's power to bear children, is said to endanger newborn babies, especially male children before they are protected by circumcision.

After this fiasco, God created the second wife from Adam's rib so that she would understand her subordinant position to her husband. The authors comment that this story "lacks parallel in Mediterranean or early Middle-Eastern myth," obviously a "myth establishing male supremacy and disguising Eve's divinity." Moreover, the authors suggest that the myth may have arisen iconotropically (that is, from misunderstanding a religious icon of an earlier culture). The icon shows the naked Goddess Anatha poised in the air, watching her lover Mot murder his twin, Aliyan. Mot (mistaken for Jehovah) is driving a curved dagger under Aliyan's fifth rib—to kill him, not to extract a sixth rib.

A bellicose reviewer protested that "in the Canaanite myth of Aliyan Baal and Mot, Baal is not in fact killed by a knife driven into his ribs. He falls as the result of a fight in which the two antagonists charge at each other like wild animals. Subsequently, he is dispatched with a falchion by Anath herself."[6] This objection does not seem to be a serious one, since Aliyan-Baal and Mot apparently destroyed each other repeatedly, often in seven-year cycles, and not all the deaths were in the same manner. Cyrus H. Gordon quotes Ugarite texts discovered in 1929 describing a whole series of such encounters between Baal and his enemies, especially Mot. In one of these Anatha kills Mot with a

sword. Mot is then planted like a seed and Baal is resurrected. Aliyan-Baal is associated with fertility; Mot with
death, drought, or otherwise infertile cycles of nature.
Anatha was likewise a fertility goddess, though she was incredibly bloodthirsty and destructive at times. Gordon
writes:

The meteorological history of Canaan, where Baal was pitted
against Mot in the minds of the people, required the concept that
the conflict between the two gods took place repeatedly. In the
frame of reference of Canaanite religious psychology each of the
two gods was both vanquished and triumphant many a time in the
course of any century. [7]

Anatha is obviously one of those goddesses who comes
under the rubric of the White Goddess, though this title is
not mentioned in the book. The material about Adam and
Eve bears the stamp of Graves's thought much more than
some other areas where Patai, the Hebrew scholar, seems to
predominate. These often bear little reference to the goddess mythology, proceeding on the usual Jewish patriarchal
assumptions.

Graves is apparently not trying to subdue the Hebrew
material to his favorite "one story only" about the twin
brothers in competition for the love of the goddess. Yet
Genesis abounds in competitive brothers: Cain and Abel,
Isaac and Ishmael, Jacob and Esau, Joseph and his brothers.
The commentaries are usually historical or traditional Hebrew ones.

There are occasional details, however, that demonstrate that the Canaanites were matrilinear: Abraham send-
ing his bond servant to Harran, for instance, to get a wife for
Isaac. Presumably, the reason he would not let Isaac marry
a Canaanite was that Isaac would then be lost to his own
clan and enter his wife's. Harran was apparently patrilinear,
allowing the bride to leave her own people and join her
husband's.

Another interesting reference to the Canaanite female

cult appears in the commentaries on the story of Jacob's two wives, Leah and Rachel, whose bride price was fourteen years of labor for his father-in-law.

The traditional order of the patriarchs' birth is that of seniority in the Leah-Rachel federation: later called 'Israel,' although at first 'Israel' properly included only the Rachel tribes. Leah ('Wild Cow') and Rachel ('Ewe'), are titles of goddesses. The wild cow is the variously named Canaanite Moon-goddess; the Ewe-goddess, mother of a Ram-god, will have been worshipped by shepherds settled in Goshen.

One of the most provocative commentaries follows the fanciful legend of the birth of Abraham, with whom Jehovah made the covenant establishing his descendants as God's Chosen People. Abraham (according to legend, not the Bible account) was born in a cave and left there to be nourished by angels, because King Nimrod was determined to destroy a child who was destined to overthrow his gods. Graves and Patai suggest that both Abraham and Jesus follow the mythic pattern of the national hero, traced by Lord Raglan in other mythologies. [8]

Lord Raglan, in *The Hero*, examines myths of many diverse heroes—Greek, Latin, Persian, Celtic and Germanic, listing their common characteristics. The hero's mother is always a princess, his reputed father a king and her near kinsman; the circumstances of his conception are unusual, and he is also reputed to be the son of a god; at his birth, an attempt is made, usually by his father or grandfather, to kill him. The hero is spirited away by his mother, reared in a far country by lowly foster-parents; nothing is known of his childhood, but on reaching manhood, he returns home, overcomes the king, sometimes also a dragon, giant or wild beast, marries a princess, often the daughter of his predecessor, and becomes king himself.

Sometimes the child is set adrift in a boat by his mother, as were Moses and Romulus; sometimes, exposed on a mountainside, as were Cyrus, Paris, and Oedipus—though Oedipus is also said to have been set adrift. The later stages of the hero's progress, his assumption of power, successful wars, and eventual tragic death, are equally constant. The myth represents a dramatic ritual in honour of the Divine Child, the fertile Spirit of the New Year. His 'advent,' which gave its name to the rites at Eleusis near Athens, was celebrated in a sacred cave, where shepherds and cattlemen carried him by torchlight. The Spirit of the New Year, in fact, defeats the Spirit of the Old Year, marries the Earth-princess, becomes King, and is himself superseded at the close of his reign.

Most reviews of the book have been respectful, with the exception of the wholly negative article by T. H. Gastor, mentioned earlier. Gastor accuses the authors of "wholesale pilfering" from Ginsburg and "thirty-one misstatements of fact."[9] One suspects that Gastor has a score to settle with Graves that rests on past works, not just *The Hebrew Myths*, for his blistering remarks seem directed entirely to Graves, with no consideration of Patai, who has written widely on Hebrew subjects. This often happens when Graves collaborates with anyone, for he is a continuing irritation to scholars who think he is invading their private territory with unorthodox interpretations.

Perhaps the most interesting comment by a reviewer is also an observation not about the book, but about Graves himself. Frank Kermode notes, as I myself have done repeatedly, the strange combination of severe rationalism and poetic consciousness that permeates Graves's prose works. Kermode says of *The Hebrew Myths* that " . . . it constitutes part of a vast encyclopaedic effort of the kind an epic poet puts in. Mr. Graves holds views on poetry which preclude his writing epics, and one imagines a sort of dissociation, an epic poet split into a writer of lyrics and epigrams on the one hand, and a curious and universal scholar on the other."[10]

My Head! My Head! (1925) is Graves's first novel and his first attempt at combining fictionalized history with his own evolving conception of reality. Already the rationalist mentality is explaining away biblical miracles, yet curiously retaining some few events that seem beyond or above reason. The novel elaborates the biblical story of Elisha and the Shunamite (II Kings, chapters 8–37) and, secondarily, through Elisha's narration, the career of Moses.

The biblical account concerning Elisha's stay in Shunem contains the barest outline of the action. Elisha and his servant Gehazi are always hospitably received when passing through Shunem by what the Bible calls a "great woman" and her husband, though the husband gets little comment. The woman has a special room built for Elisha that is always available for his rest and refreshment. Elisha wishes to return some favor for such hospitality. Gehazi tells his master that the Shunamite yearns for a child, but her husband is old. Therefore, Elisha tells her she will bear a son.

One day when the "child was grown," as the Bible puts it, he goes out to the fields where his father is superintending the reapers. He suddenly cries out to his father, "My Head! My Head!" One of the workers carries him to his mother, and he soon dies in his mother's arms. The Shunamite lays the boy on Elisha's bed, procures an ass, and rides in haste to Mount Carmel where Elisha is. Elisha hurries back with the woman, lies down on top of the boy, with his mouth upon the boy's mouth, his eyes upon his eyes, his hands upon his hands. Gradually warmth returns to the body and the boy revives.

The same Shunamite woman is mentioned later in II Kings, chapter eight, when Elisha predicts a famine and tells the Shunamite to take her son and leave the district for seven years. She stays in the land of the Philistines for that length of time, then comes back and appeals to the king for the return of her house and lands. When the king finds out that this is the woman whose son Elisha reclaimed from death, he restores all that was hers. The shadowy husband is never mentioned in this part of the story. This later episode is not a part of Graves's novel. Like the first encounter, however, it seems to leave much unsaid.

In the Preface to *My Head! My Head!*, Graves said he was discussing the Shunamite woman with the daughter of an Anglican Archdeacon at a tea party. His companion

suggested that Elisha was the father of the child and that
Elisha had first hypnotized her. Just why the hypnotism is
added is not clear, though it would conveniently preserve
both the lady's conscience from a knowledge of adultery and
Elisha's reputation as a holy man. Graves raised the question whether the Shunamite was a serious temptation to
Elisha or whether he was simply arranging for the child she
desired. They decided that Elisha's conscience was not entirely clear, because he could not read her thoughts when
she came to him on Mount Carmel. In the Bible, Elisha
says ". . . her soul is vexed within her: and the Lord hath
held it from me, and hath not told me." The implication is
that he should have known intuitively what was in her
mind. Graves proposes that Elisha's inability to read her
mind suggests something unclean in their relationship,
from Elisha's point of view.

From these rather flimsy clues, Graves constructs a
story wherein both Elisha and his servant Gehazi break their
vows of celibacy. Elisha himself has ambiguous motives for
his "service" to Jochebed, the Shunamite woman, for he
secretly loves her, yet wishes to preserve her virtue, and
wants to provide her with a child. Moreover, Elisha carries
a certain guilt for the seduction of Gehazi by Jochebed's
maid Zibiah, for Elisha has been told that his follower will
keep his vows only so long as Elisha does.[11]

The novel demonstrates both Graves's rational tendency to explain miracles in naturalistic terms and his contrary fascination with a certain suprarational possibility for
special persons. Though the engendering of the child is
perfectly understandable, no attempt is made to explain his
resurrection in equally realistic terms. The child possibly
suffered a heat stroke and may have been in a coma, yet he
showed all the signs of death.

There is considerable discussion about the nature of
"miracles." The holy man is, among other things, an accomplished shaman. He can produce illusions like any
good magician—and did, indeed, according to Graves,

hypnotize Jochebed in order to impregnate her without her knowledge. This does not mean that he was at all insincere in his motives under most circumstances. Moreover, through his faith in Jah (Jehovah), he was capable of controlling reality in a seemingly miraculous way, though at great expense of nervous and emotional energy.

There seems to be some emotional law of the conservation of energy even in magic. One reason why the holy man fasts, prays, and lives a very austere life is to store up a potential for prophecy and miracle. Some deeds exact a dreadful toll. In fact, Elisha knows that saving the life of Jochebed's child involves giving his own in its place. He prays for the boon of nine months more of life, the same that the child spent in the womb.[12] This prayer is granted.

Graves's curious views on magic are not entirely consistent with his debunking of miracles. In later novels, Graves almost invariably used a first person narrator. This protects the writer from charges of idiosyncratic views, even when one suspects the narrator is speaking for his creator. The Elisha story, however, is told from an omniscient point of view. Moreover, the Preface clearly implies that Graves is trying to make a plausible case for what might really have happened.

He uses the idea of a life forfeited for a life returned in *King Jesus* two decades later, in the case of Jesus raising Lazarus from the dead. But that story is told from the point of view of a narrator who might well believe in the supernatural. In *The Nazarene Gospel Restored*, written presumably from a scholarly viewpoint, the writers (Graves and Podro) simply deny that Jesus raised Lazarus from the dead. Thus, the miraculous giving life for life is apparently a literary device, not really an attempt to reconstruct reality. The reviewer in the *Spectator* demonstrated some exasperation on this point:

As a romancer Mr. Graves is acceptable enough. As a theorist, however, he has embarked upon stormy seas with too frail a craft. Does he really imagine, for example, that he has 'faced squarely'

the question of miracles, which he partly whittles down by
rationalistic explanations, and partly supports by his own not very
plausible ideas on magic? This compromise may satisfy Mr.
Graves himself. But it is not likely to convince many of his
readers.[13]

The novel has a second story within the story of Elisha
and the Shunamite. Jochebed is a very intelligent woman
and questions Elisha eagerly about the life of Moses. Elisha
obligingly offers to teach Jochebed and her husband, Issachar. But Issachar is a stolid, conventional man who
memorizes scripture without questioning it, and prefers to
deal with husbandry and the crops. Therefore, Jochebed,
chaperoned by her maid, sits at the feet of the master and
listens to the story of Moses.

Graves had an extensive biblical account to draw on
here. He improvised quite freely on the main elements of
the story. He makes Moses more human than the biblical
hero, and not above using a few magician's tricks of his own
to impress both his own people and the Egyptians. Practically all miracles are explained in naturalistic terms.

Moses' Ethiopian wife, who corresponds regularly
with her relatives, gives him advance information that
allows him to foresee certain natural disasters. These he
duly prophesies to Pharoah as evidence of Jah's wrath. She
tells him, for instance, that her father reports a deadly red
growth clogging the springs that feed the Nile. When the
floods wash this substance down to Egypt, the land will be
sick. Thus, Moses calculates the time for the next flooding
of the Nile and tells Pharoah that Jah will turn the Nile to
blood. Most of the other plagues that Moses uses to force
Pharoah to release the Israelites occur as a natural sequence
of events stemming from the initial poisoning of the river
life by this substance. In each case, Moses observes what is
happening in the ecosystem of the river and foresees the
next development.

When his father-in-law says that his tribe has frightened
off a plague of locusts with much noise, but they are headed
down the river, Moses immediately prophesies that Jah will

send locusts. He meanwhile instructs the Hebrews to be ready with noise makers to deflect the locusts as much as possible from their own fields. The threatened murder, presumably by Jah's angel of death, of eldest sons in every Egyptian household, is really perpetrated by specially trained Hebrew assassins dressed in black. (Whether it is more justifiable for God to murder children than it is for humans to do so is, perhaps, a moot point.)

Moses is, in many respects, an unhappy man. He is forced to kill his Ethiopian wife, the only woman he ever loved, because the Hebrews think she is a witch. He is always more feared than loved, for the people often hate him for letting them wander in the desert for forty years instead of leading them directly into the Promised Land. Yet this terrible hardship is a necessary preliminary to the conquest of that very land they dream of. Moses knows that the passive slaves he led out of Egypt could never conquer the trained warriors of free nations. He waited until the younger generation could be trained to a new, rugged, warrior discipline. Not until the last moment did his people realize the necessity of their long and painful trial or recognize the true stature of Moses' hard and sometimes merciless leadership.

This novel demonstrates for the first time Graves's lifelong interest in the beginnings of western civilization and the changing relationships between men and women. He must have already read some of the nineteenth century anthropologists, probably Briffault and Bachofen, who posited an initial stage of promiscuity where women were the only cohesive center of culture. Elisha describes this state of affairs when he begins his story of Moses.

"Now in the early generations of men it was hidden from the wise what is known now even to fools that a child is only born to a woman by reason of a man first knowing her carnally. . . . There was no husband then and no wife and no father, only the mother; and her children, men and women, embraced without marriage and without dowry as the birds do and the beasts.

"In those days was the beginning of religion in Egypt and

woman was held to be of the gods and sacred because she was possessed of those ghosts whom she bore as children: the mother ruled and all the possessions of the family were the mother's right. Latterly men perceived that though there were some women who were barren and some impotent to beget children, yet no woman conceived unless she had first known a man carnally. Then man began to boast himself and say: 'If it were not for the man, no child would be born, we can give and we can withhold. . . .' Thus the mother lost her rule in the family and the father assumed it easily, for he was of greater bodily strength. Then was the beginning of our present misery when woman was despised and put in subjection to man. . . ."

Graves also conjectures on the nature of gods in this novel, a minor theme that yet reappears over and over in later work. He has written a satirical "Autobiography of Baal." "Baal," he explains, was one of God's aliases. In the Claudius novels, the Emperor Claudius suggests that gods exist because people worship them. Thus, Augustus, and even the treacherous Livia, can indeed become gods by proclamation and subsequent worship. In the last analysis, perhaps, the peculiar reality of gods has involved Graves's ambiguous attitude toward the White Goddess as a necessity for the poetic imagination and yet, in some sense, an independent reality. In *My Head! My Head!*, Jochebed asks, "Who then is Jah?" Elisha answers:

"He is the God of the Hebrews and without the Hebrews He is nothing. If the Hebrews embrace other peoples and they also come to believe on Jah, then He is the God also of these other peoples. But His strength is no greater than the strength of His people. If the Hebrews multiply and spread over the earth so that all other nations perish before Jah, then, and not until then, is Jah all-powerful, for other nations have their own gods and by them do their own wonders and from them receive their own ordinances."

The Shunamite said: "Is the people then the God?"

Elisha answered: "No, not more than a man's father or mother or his children are himself. They are of him or to him, but they are not the man himself."

Is the analogy to parents and children misleading?

These relationships are rooted in the material world, then develop spiritual overtones. Perhaps Graves is suggesting that the existential principle "existence precedes essence" applies to gods as well as man. Graves has never shown any interest in existentialism however, nor used its images. Jean Paul Sartre, French existentialist, said that there is no such thing as "human nature," that human beings first exist, then create their nature by what they do. Thus, human nature is simply what men choose. In this case, god's nature is not what he himself chooses, apparently, but what his worshippers choose. He may begin crudely in some primitive fear or raw power or a desperate appeal for protection. As his worshippers become more refined in perception and aspiration, god loses his brutishness and acquires spirituality and holiness. Actually, this accords with scholarly perceptions of the evolution of the god concept in the Old Testament from a tribal war god to a universal god of mercy and justice. What Graves seems to be suggesting in addition is that a god, at any stage of its development, is a very real source of magical power for his priest or prophet.

Another issue that interested Graves is the degree to which knowledge of past and future depends upon an understanding of the present. Jochebed is quite satisfied that Elisha has the past "spread out like an open book," but how can anyone prophesy the future, which does not yet exist? Elisha explains that she foretells the future every day with more or less success, saying that it is going to rain or that her husband is going to do such and such when he comes home. "That knowledge you had was not knowledge of the future" he says, "for no knowledge is so, but it is a knowledge of things happening in the present time. So also with knowledge of the past."

The prophecies made by us prophets are in general clearer than the prophecies of other men because, being prophets, we live retired from private quarrels and envies and greed so that our knowledge, as men say, of the future, though this is truly knowledge of the present, is unclouded with those hopes and fears which confuse the truth. We can forecast very nearly how any event will

turn, where our advantage is not privately touched by this knowledge, yet our knowledge of the thing before it comes is always a
great way removed from our knowledge of the thing after it has
been."

In this discussion of past and future as only knowable
through the present, there is at least a foreshadowing of the
method that Graves called analeptic, by which he immersed
himself so deeply in a particular past and a particular historical personage, that he could presumably fill in the gaps of
history by sheer power of intuition. He celebrated this imaginative grasp of the past as though it were the living present
in a poem entitled "To Bring the Dead to Life."

> To bring the dead to life
> Is no great magic.
> Few are wholly dead:
> Blow on a dead man's embers
> And a live flame will start.
>
> Let his forgotten griefs be now,
> And now his withered hopes;
> Subdue your pen to his handwriting
> Until it prove as natural
> To sign his name as yours.

The writer must assume the dead person's opinions, his way
of walking, his habits and preferences. But this "resurrection" of the dead exacts a penalty—one very similar to
Elisha's for resurrecting Jochebed's son:

> So grant him life, but reckon
> That the grave which housed him
> May not be empty now:
> You in his spotted garments
> Shall yourself be wrapped.

Yet Graves has not really entered into the character of
the Hebrew prophet, at least in Elisha's interpretation of
Moses. The story of Elisha and Jochebed is touching and
human. But the story of Moses, though well told and more

plausible to a modern mind than the original, seems hardly the voice of a Hebrew prophet. To be sure, one can never be sure how sophisticated the ancients might have been about wonderworking, their own and others. It seems unlikely, however, that Elisha, upon whose shoulders the mantle of Elijah dropped from heaven, would expound on sacred heroes like a benign English philosopher. Surely, only Abraham, the father of the faith, could command more reverence than Moses. Elisha would not have much empathy, I suspect, for Graves's compromise of, say, twenty percent magic to eighty percent empiricism. Graves learned to handle this difficulty more plausibly in later novels.

8

Search for the Historical Jesus:
The Nazarene Gospel Restored

While *The Hebrew Myths: The Book of Genesis* reveals the wealth of myth that surrounds the Old Testament, *The Nazarene Gospel Restored* seeks to demythologize the historical Jesus. Graves collaborated with Joshua Podro to produce this impressive tome (982 pages). The authors explore the ways the original Nazarene tradition has become distorted. The Foreword lists three reasons why the story has changed: editorial carelessness or misunderstanding, doctrinal piety or perversity, and polemical shrewdness.

Under each of these three categories of error, which sometimes overlap, they list nine or ten specific applications. Under carelessness appear such items as misunderstanding of the Aramaic original, running sayings together into a single confused argument, misinterpreting sacred pictures. The authors claim complete originality only for the latter of these. Doctrinal piety accounts for converting Jesus' symbolic acts into miracles, inventing miracles or sayings that would support second-century church practice, substituting "I" for "God" in many of his sayings. Polemical shrewdness inspired many gross misrepresentations—the attempts to prove that Jesus flouted the Mosaic Law, that he debarred the Jews from the Kingdom of Heaven in favor of gentiles, that he despised the Pharisees, that the Jews were responsible for his death (an error only recently acknowledged by the Roman Catholic church).

Considering that Jesus himself, though a learned man

in Jewish tradition, did not write down his own story or teachings, and those who did do so were far removed from him in time and even in language, distortion was inevitable. What emerges from the work of Graves and Podro is a more credible historical Jesus who deserves the respect and admiration of persons who, for intellectual reasons, have rejected the supernatural Christ.

Most contemporary believers probably do not realize the extent of the confusion and disagreement about basic principles that beset the early church. As to the authorship of the gospels, the Foreword says:

Gospels written by members of the various Gentile Churches, after the Destruction of the Temple in 70 A.D., to support local doctrine, were piously attributed to the Apostles Matthew, John, James the Less, Peter, Thomas, Bartholomew, Andrew, and 'The Twelve'. Of these, the first two alone, with the addition of *Luke* and *Mark*, have become canonical, and then only after continuous drastic revision. Of the rest, some survive whole, some in part, some have been suppressed as heretical; and fragments of several other named and unnamed Gospels are extant. But none of these, whether canonical or uncanonical, can have been written by the author to whom it is ascribed. The introduction to *Luke* and the account quoted by Eusebius from the early second-century writer Papias . . . show that all the Gospels, except the patently fictitious ones, were based on notes taken by Greek-speaking converts from the Aramaic Gospel orally current among the Nazarenes; and that each evangelist, as Papias reports: 'interpreted them as best he could'—that is to say, uncritically and, in general, with studied ignorance of their historical background.

Jesus's teaching, the authors point out, was usually delivered in the form of *midrashim,* or commentaries—that is, he would quote a scriptural text and apply it to a contemporary occasion (as in Luke xiv, 8–10, where his parable is based on Proverbs xxv, 6–7; or Matthew v, 25, where he expands Proverbs xxv, 8–9). Yet Greek editors who wished to show Jesus as original in his teachings would omit the introductory quotation.

St. Paul, who never knew Jesus personally, concocted a religion *about Christ*, presumably offering a "new dispensation" by God for man's salvation. He could not allow Jesus to be a Jewish prophet and purifier of Jewish moral law, in the traditional path of the old testament prophets, speaking for God but never claiming to be God.

It is clear, from *Matthew* v. 18..., that Jesus considered the Law so sacred and immutable that none who transgressed the least of its ordinances might hope to partake of God's Kingdom. Also, that Paul makes only scanty reference in his Epistles to the life and teaching of Jesus; that he came into sharp conflict with the Twelve, whose view of the Law was diametrically opposed to his; and that the texts of all the Canonical Gospels have been manipulated in favour of the Pauline view.

Less than thirty years after Jesus was crucified, the early church split into three factions who bitterly quarreled with each other over matters of doctrine. The Nazarene Church, headed by James the Just and Jesus's other disciples, continued to obey the Pharisaic Sanhedrin, the central authority of orthodox Jewish doctrine. The "Grecian" churches of Egypt and Libya were largely controlled by the Gnostics, who believed that matter is evil and that emancipation comes through immediate knowledge of spiritual truth attained through faith alone.

The Gentile Churches of Greece, Asia Minor, and Italy, however, were controlled by Paul, who sought to purge Christianity of its distinctive Jewishness. To this impulse, the authors ascribe the impression that the Pharisees seem to be antagonists to Jesus in the gospels. "Pharisee," which has acquired the meaning in Christian tradition of "pompous hypocrite," originally meant "separated," referring to a person who dedicated himself to religious purity. Jesus never discredited the Pharisees as a group, but condemned hypocritical Pharisees who fell short of their ideals. Like the prophets before him, he exhorted religious leaders to practice what they preach. Moreover, he upheld the religious authority of the Great Sanhedrin (*Matthew* xxiii,

27): "The scribes and Pharisees sit in Moses's seat. All therefore they bid you observe, that observe and do." Jesus was not a revolutionary against Jewish tradition. The authors write, "Jesus's message was simple: that the Day of Judgment described in great detail by the prophets Zechariah, Zephaniah, Malachi and others, was at hand, and that all must repent and prepare for the coming trials."

It was not until the second century that the Pharisees began to distrust the Nazarenes for their belief in Jesus as the Messiah—a doctrine also held by the clearly heretical Paulines, who threatened the very existence of the synagogue system and basic Jewish requirements, such as circumcision and food restrictions. "After discarding all Jewish ritual observances, even the ban on food that had been offered to idols . . ., the Gentile Christians equated Jesus with one aspect of God . . . namely His Word, or the expression of His Mind, and transformed Jesus's teachings into a Greek mystery-cult." This was blasphemy, from the Nazarene point of view. The Nazarene sect managed to retain its identity until the fifth century, when some returned to more orthodox Judaism, while others capitulated to the gentile church.

What the Jews meant by the Messiah is quite different from what it has come to mean to gentile Christians. The Messiah was to be a servant of God, like Moses or David or Elijah, but not an aspect of God. He might have God-given supernatural attributes, in that some thought he would be raised from the dead and rule in Jerusalem for a thousand years. But this was to be a purified earthly kingdom, where God's people would be united at last. This "Son of David" was:

. . . the pastoral king foretold by Ezekiel, by the author of Psalms xvii and xviii, by Zechariah and Malachi, by the author of the Psalter of Solomon, by Esdras, and by many others. He would be born of a young mother in Judean Bethlehem . . . after a period crowded with wars, famines, and natural calamities, the so-called Pangs of the Messiah, when the Jews were floundering in a slough of misery. He would be summoned from an obscure home and

anointed King by the ever-young Elijah. . . . Elijah was to prepare
the way for the Messiah, who would thereupon enter Jerusalem
riding in triumph on a young ass.

Though the pacifistic Jesus could hardly play the role
of the Warrior Messiah, who would defeat the enemies of
Israel in a final war, his followers identified him as the
anointed prophet foretold in Zechariah and Deuteronomy,
who would be the Suffering Servant, a scapegoat figure,
who would take upon himself all his people's sins, and thus
inaugurate the Messianic Kingdom. The Suffering Servant,
representing the whole nation of Israel, must be "a marred,
uncomely, despised man, reckoned a sinner, sentenced to
dishonourable death, dumb before his accusers, and hurried
by them to the grave. . . ." He would attain his victory
after his death.

There was a rival concept to the Son of David. He was
called the Son of Joseph, or the Son of Ephraim, another
warlike Messiah, who was to rule over the ten tribes of the
North. The Son of David cult centered in Jerusalem, while
the Son of Joseph cult thought that the royal sceptre would
pass from the tribe of Judah to a Josephite, since Jacob had
prophesied that from Joseph (that is, the Old Testament
patriarch, not the carpenter father of Jesus) would spring the
Shepherd, the Rock of Israel.

A third conception of the Messiah was the Son of
Man, derived from Daniel vii. He seems to be a more
supernatural concept. He is to ride into Jerusalem not on an
ass, but on a storm cloud. Some thought that he was a
heavenly spirit who would follow a parallel action to the
earthly Messiah.

A fourth Messiah was to be a priest-king of the tribe of
Levi, supported by a Judean general. His claims are advanced in the uncanonical *Testament of Levi*. He would
sanctify the conquests of his general, bring universal peace,
and cleanse the people of their sins.

Most of the book is devoted to collecting and compar-
ing all the accounts of particular biblical episodes, along

with apocryphal material or early commentaries on the event. These quotes are followed with a discussion of textual difficulties, probable errors or changes, inconsistencies between what is known historically of the period and what is recorded in the gospels. The authors try to account logically for the changes, often attributing them to the ignorance or misplaced piety of gentile followers of Paul's brand of Christianity. Some of Jesus's sayings are presumed to be out of context. The Pharisaic method of cataloging sayings was by subject, rather than chronology, which may give credence to such a jumbling of messages.

Various naturalistic explanations are offered for the miracles attributed to Jesus. The authors claim that Jesus did not, in fact, raise Lazarus from the dead, though he may have tried to. Such a spectacular event would not have been neglected by the evangelists, yet only the Gospel of John details the story. In the case of the miraculous turning of water into wine, when the wedding party ran out of refreshment, the authors suggest that this was simply a moral parable, perfectly understood by the guests, if not by subsequent literalists. Jesus, in offering them water, is suggesting that the "wine of the spirit" is better than strong drink.

The authors also believe that Jesus did not die on the cross, though he was in profound shock from his experiences. They are by no means the first to suggest this possibility. In an article called "Jewish Jesus . . . Gentile Christ,"[1] Graves comments on George Moore's book about Jesus, *The Brook Kerith*. Graves did not like Moore, but he gives him credit for three "bold and, I think, accurate guesses": "That Paul willfully misrepresented Jesus; that Jesus survived the Cross; and that he then considered himself to have offended God by 'forcing the hour'—these seem to me logically inescapable conclusions." Samuel Butler's *Fair Haven* also argued for the literal survival of Jesus after his crucifixion.

Graves and Podro credibly remove some of the usual objections to this explanation. One reason for Graves's willingness to entertain this rational view, however, is a personal one: his own "death" during World War I, which he recounts in a footnote. On that occasion, a doctor mistook complete anaesthesia for death, and Graves lay in profound shock for twenty-four hours awaiting burial, before he moved and someone noticed. Graves apologizes for introducing autobiographical material into the argument, but it shows that such things can indeed happen. There is, indeed, one recorded instance of a man surviving crucifixion.

One of the most ingenious, or some might say, tortuous speculations in this book is the complicated discussion of what the authors call the coronation of Jesus as king of the Jews. This ritual, performed by John the Baptist, involved possibly a rebirth ceremony from a temple virgin (therefore, rebirth symbolically of God) and even a marriage to Mary, the sister of Martha and Lazarus.

The notion of Jesus's marrying may not be so clearly explained in this volume as it is in Graves's novel *King Jesus*. Jesus is sometimes referred to in the Bible as a bridegroom, a term later used metaphorically in relation to the Christian church as Christ's bride—a notion foreign, of course, to the Jews of Jesus' time. (The Jews might have thought of Israel as Christ's bride.) In the novel, however, Graves made it clear that ownership of the land was matrilinear, passed on from mother to youngest daughter. Therefore the king must marry the inheritor of the land to legitimize his claim. That is why, Graves wrote, King David married a daughter of each of the tribes of Israel, in order to unite the tribes under one rule. It also accounts for the incestuous brother-sister marriages among Egyptian pharaohs. Nonetheless, it is questionable whether female ownership of the land was still a live custom in Jesus' day. Even if it were not, one could at least imagine Jesus wishing to enact all traditional rituals associated with kingship.

In any case, Jesus presumably refused to consummate his marriage, if such occurred. Graves and Podro explain

Jesus' asceticism thus in *Jesus in Rome*, an epilogue to *The Nazarene Gospel Restored:* "Sexual connection disabled a man for three days and nights from the achievement of perfect holiness (Exodus xix, 15; Samuel xxi, 1–6), and Jesus' recommendation that his disciples should make themselves eunuchs for the Kingdom of Heaven's sake (Matthew xxix, 12) can have been intended only as an insurance of their perfect holiness when the Day of the Lord suddenly dawned." There is ample evidence in the Bible that Jesus expected that day of judgment very soon indeed.

The authors quote Dr. Raphael Patai's *Hebrew Installation Rites*[2] about the rites involved in crowning a king. Patai reveals that the entering of the spirit of God into the newly annointed king closely corresponds to ancient ceremonies symbolizing death and rebirth of the king. The theory is that the king must die, then is reborn as a god. There are traces, Patai says, of this theory in the Hebrew installation ritual.

Graves and Podro add that the king's mother is important also in this ceremony. Solomon, they point out, had two mothers, a physical one and an adoptive one (presumably acquired when he became king of Israel.) Symbolic rebirth from a Levite temple virgin would not only give credence to the notion of virgin birth by a divine Father, but also enable Jesus, through Joseph a son of David, to assume also the role of the Levite priest-king, which was one of the prevailing concepts of the Messiah.

The Nazarenes would fear to reveal this ritual to Romans, however, even Roman converts. Since Rome had established the house of Herod on the throne (without benefit of anointing in the Old Testament style), such a traditional return would suggest sedition—even though Jesus was interested only in a spiritual kingdom. The Nazarenes, therefore, fragmented the story of the ritual and scattered it in other contexts throughout the gospels.

Graves and Podro then suggest several startling re-readings of biblical episodes. The Annunciation of the

Virgin Mary is thus misplaced, not heralding the physical birth of Jesus from Joseph's wife, but rather summoning a temple virgin (symbolically, God's spouse) to become an adoptive mother to an anointed king, who thereafter would be "God's beloved Son." And the occasion after Jesus' arrest, when the Roman soldiers supposedly dressed Jesus in royal purple, crowned him with thorns, then scourged and mocked him before leading him off to die, may really have been part of the symbolic purifying ceremony a king was subjected to before being reborn as God's anointed. Though attributed to the Romans, it was presumably Jesus' own followers who scourged him at the time of his coronation.

This reader cannot help perceiving that here, as in *The White Goddess*, Graves, at least, is again preoccupied with literary puzzles and esoteric secrets, presumably waiting through the centuries for just such an intuitive reconstruction. This is not to say that such a reading is necessarily implausible. The truth of the matter will probably never be known.

This work tends, to be sure, to place Jesus in a plausible historical context, instead of a supernatural one. Nor is the notion that Jesus deliberately reenacted prophecies or Old-Testament rituals at all unreasonable. The fact that Jesus chose to ride into Jerusalem on an ass, for instance, indicates his conscious choosing of a prophesied role for the Messiah. This kind of deliberate role-playing is not at all fraudulent, but neither is it necessarily a supernatural working out of God-ordained destiny.

That the gospels undoubtedly suffered considerable distortion seems undeniable, given the manner of their recording and the fallibility of humans. One can hardly depend upon yesterday's account of the news, let alone the confusing religious records of a bygone age. That Graves and Podro have always, or even most of the time, guessed correctly in trying to unscramble the mysteries and inconsistencies of the gospels seems questionable. Yet they have explored the text, the historical background, the history of ancient religions with a thoroughness unrivaled, I suspect, by 90 percent of today's priests and theologians. Anyone interested in the Bible either historically or religiously should find this volume fascinating—provided, of course, they can consider heretical interpretation without rancor.

As anyone might expect, Graves and Podro received a wave of bad reviews from the devout when this book was published. Some even led to lawsuits and forced retractions on the part of reviewers. Only one prominent theologian, Reinhold Niebuhr, praised the volume: "A work of careful scholarship. The authors have laboured so diligently and so honestly, that the volume will be of great service to both Jews and Christians."

As Graves and Podro pointed out in *Jesus in Rome,* even though a large proportion of Christians have ceased to believe in biblical miracles, books on Christian subjects are always given to orthodox Christians to review. Moses Hadas in the *New York Times,* however, correctly described the method and probable effect of the book, and tolerantly chides hysterical reactions:

Though there is much learning in this book, its strength, like its weaknesses, is in its imaginative aspects, and its approach (though not its close and systematic treatment) is analogous to that of Graves' 'Claudius' novels. There, too, evidence which professional scholars had rejected was made to support an ingenious reconstruction. But where traditionalists might smile at Graves' temerity in rehabilitating a pagan emperor whom the ancients denigrated, they will be outraged by this revolutionary reconstruction of sacred history and apprehensive of the harm it might cause. Apprehensions on this score are surely baseless. [3]

Another critic, H. J. McLachilian, deplores the process of guessing when the evidence is really inconclusive. This criticism certainly has merit from a strictly scholarly point of view, though it may rest on an unreliable assumption that "real historians" have some dependable, scientific way to discover the truth. McLachilian says:

Considerable erudition, in particular a wide knowledge of the Rabbinical literature, has gone into the making of this book, but the misapplication of learning in defence of an extremely improbable thesis is unfortunately a commonplace of this particular field of studies and Messrs Graves and Podro are not above criticism on this score. A great deal of their exegesis is forced, and no amount of learning or shrewd guesswork can compensate for a careful weighing of evidence and the confession that, where evidence is lacking or inadequate, the only honest conclusion is to say, "We do not know!"[4]

Graves and Podro point out in *Jesus in Rome* that any document that seemed to weaken orthodox Christianity, faced rejection, at this time, for political, as well as religious reasons:

Of the two most powerful military alliances in the world today, one is predominantly Christian; the other, predominantly God-less. Their opposition makes our task invidious. Any reasoned study of Christian origins which questions the historical dogmas of the Roman and Protestant Churches is likely to be either dismissed as fanciful or censured as wilfully weakening the morale that binds the 'Free World' together. Thus our *Nazarene Gospel Restored* (London and New York, 1954) was rudely rejected by almost every Protestant reviewer in Britain and the United States (a singular exception being Reinhold Niebuhr, the theologian); politely if cautiously received by Jewish scholars, who preferred not to take sides in an argument on this, to them, painful subject; and wholly disregarded by the Roman Catholics, perhaps in acknowledgment of our having conceded the logical tenability of their position— granted certain supernatural axioms. Since we had pointed out that the Protestants, by not insisting on such axioms as a matter of Church discipline, were encouraging historical doubts which they could not lay at rest. It was only to be expected that their general reaction to *The Nazarene Gospel Restored* would be abuse, misrepresentation, and a scornful rejection of our scholarly credentials.

It should be clear that *The Nazarene Gospel Restored* is by no means contemptuous or in any way disrespectful to

Jesus (Paul is somewhat diminished, to be sure—actually, in support of Jesus.) The authors seek to present Jesus as they believe he really was: a gentle and righteous man who tried to be the prophesied savior of the Jews. The last 178 pages of the volume offer the Nazarene Gospel rewritten as the authors suppose it might have been originally. It is more plausible, in some ways, than the biblical version, and eloquent in its own right.

Whether or not general readers will find this book useful or interesting depends heavily upon two things: First, can they comfortably entertain unorthodox interpretations of scripture? And second, can they allow an author the faults of his virtues? He who ventures in the imagination beyond the provable facts (as Graves, at least, almost always does) will no doubt err, but he may also discover a fresh perspective on a time-worn subject.

9

King Jesus

If any prospective reader of *King Jesus* supposes that Robert
Graves strips Jesus of his Christian aura of supernaturalism
and thus "explains" him rationally to the skeptical modern
reader; or, on the other hand, if any believer supposes that
he can read this book comfortably without setting aside
some of the most cherished traditions of Christianity, let
such readers beware. This is not a book for those easily
offended by unorthodox views—nor is it a book for those
who wish to secularize Jesus into an uncomplicated teacher
of morals. Robert Graves's Jesus is literally the King of the
Jews, the grandson of Herod, who aspired to bring his
people into a new golden age of the spirit.

The novel is also Graves's most controversial application of his theory that Mediterranean peoples were initially
worshipers of the Great Triple Goddess, whom he usually
calls the White Goddess, while the male gods were originally sons, consorts, and ritual sacrifices to the Great Goddess. They emerged as independent gods only with considerable difficulty. Jehovah, also, according to Graves, was
once called a devoted son of the Great Goddess. In fact, he
formed a trinity with two of the Goddess's three persons,
namely, Anatha of the Lions and Ashima of the Doves, the
counterparts of Juno and Minerva (or Hera and Athene
among the Greeks). The remaining person, a kind of Hecate named Sheol, ruled the infernal regions. The book of
the Prophet Ezekiel contains Jehovah's bill of divorcement

from his two Goddess-partners, there called Aholah and Aholibah.

As a matter of fact, the main adversary to Jesus is not Herod the King, who sought to destroy the infant Jesus, or the Devil, who tempted him in the wilderness, or Pontius Pilate, who let him be crucified with no evidence of guilt, or Judas Iscariot, who betrayed him to the Romans. His adversary is the Goddess herself. As Graves's narrator of this strange history of the wonder-worker Jesus explains:

Nobody can understand the story of Jesus except in the light of this Jewish obsession of celestial patriarchy; for it must never be forgotten that, despite all appearances, despite even his apparent sponsorship of the Eucharistical rite, Jesus was true to Jehovah from his childhood onward without a single lapse in loyalty. He once told Shelom, the midwife who had brought him into the world, that he had "come to destroy the work of the female"; he accepted the title of "Son of David"—King David who had stabilized the Jewish monarchy and persuaded the priestesses of Anatha, until then the proud rulers of clans and tribes, to content themselves with membership of his royal harem. And as the Second Adam, Jesus's self-imposed task was to undo the evil which, according to the patriarchal legend, the First Adam had caused by sinfully listening to the seductive plea of his wife Eve.

Though this book touches upon or amplifies most of the important acts of Jesus, as recorded in the gospels, many incidents are changed significantly, presumably as a result of Graves's meticulous investigation of other sources of information about the current beliefs, customs and stories of the time. Graves writes in the Historical Commentary at the end of the novel: "A detailed commentary written to justify the unorthodox views contained in this book would be two or three times as long as the book itself, and would take years to complete; I beg to be excused the task." As a matter of fact, however, seven years later Graves and Joshua Podro published *The Nazarene Gospel Restored*, almost a thousand pages in length, trying to recapture the historical Jesus, or at least the version of his life that was current among his

original followers. That account differs from the fictionalized *King Jesus* in a number of ways.

There are probably many who have doubted the im-
maculate conception of Jesus as literal Son of God and have
speculated about the possibility that he was fathered by
Joseph, Mary's husband, or even that he might have been
illegitimate. In *The Nazarene Gospel Restored*, Graves and
Podro claim that gentile Christians first tolerated, then encouraged the "Hellenistic notion" that Jesus had been
spiritually begotten by God. It excited the horror of Pales-
tinian Jews, the authors say, and the ridicule of Romans
and Greeks, who concluded that Jesus was a bastard.

In Graves's novel Jesus is challenged in the temple,
when still a boy, because the priests discover that he was
born before the date of Joseph's final payment of the marriage debt to the high priest. Until that payment, Mary's
relationship to Joseph was betrothal, not marriage. It was
expressly forbidden by Jewish law for any bastard to enter
the inner confines of the temple. Since Mary had not yet
explained to Jesus the unusual circumstances of his birth,
this apparent taint is a profound shock to the budding prophet, whose sensitive knowledge of the law already exceeds
that of the learned elders who question him.

From that moment the brilliant mind of the young
Jesus, so eager for knowledge and already intuitively prophetic, suffers an eclipse of several years. This presumably
accounts for the curious blank in biblical accounts concerning most of Jesus' early years. In Graves's novel, anyway,
Jesus suffers in silence these doubts about his legitimacy. In
his early manhood, however, Mary reveals the amazing
story of his royal birth, the only offspring of a secret marriage between Mary and Antipater, the eldest son of Herod,
King of Israel.

To explain this fairytale relationship is unusually complex, even for Graves, but here are the bare bones of the
argument. In the first place, the dominant religion of the
Israelites, the cult of Jehovah, attained supremacy over ear-

lier female deities. Yet, Mary, the mother of Jesus, is indirectly associated with the moon goddess, as are some of the other key female characters. In the first section of the novel, pious Joachim of the House of Eli, one of the so-called Heirs of David, receives a welcome prophecy from the Canaanite chieftain that his wife Hannah, who has been barren, would present him with a child. When Joachim asks if it would be male or female, the seer answers thus:

"Who can prophesy whether the Sun or the Moon was first created? But if the Sun, then let him be called the Sun's name, Herahmeel; and if the Moon, then let her be called by the Moon's name, Miriam."

"Is the Moon named Miriam among you?"

"The Moon has many names among our poets. She is Lilith and Eve and Ashtaroth and Rahab and Tamar and Leah and Rachel and Michal and Anatha; but she is Miriam when her star rises in love from the salt sea at evening."

Some of these names are of Old Testament women, suggesting that they were considered (at least by the Canaanites) incarnations of the moon goddess. Others such as Ashtaroth and Anatha, were pagan goddesses. Lilith, as previously mentioned, was the first wife of Adam, who refused to submit to her husband's domination. She fled from Adam, according to legend, and coupled with the devil instead, begetting demons. Jehovah, faced with this unpleasant miscarriage of his plans for the Garden of Eden, made sure that Eve, Adam's second wife, would know her proper place by forming her from Adam's rib, instead of from the dust as he did Adam and Lilith. Most references to Lilith have been carefully removed from the canon of holy books, but she lives on in popular legend as the first witch. One might note that the evening star mentioned in the passage, "she is Miriam when her star rises in love from the salt sea at evening," must be the planet Venus, another aspect of the great pagan goddess of birth, love, and death.

Hannah's child, prophesied by the Canaanite, Miriam or Mary, becomes one of the vestal virgins of the temple at

Jerusalem, and therefore a ward of Simon, the High Priest. Simon reveals to Antipater, pious and gentle son of the tyrannical Herod, that in Israel every ancient king has ruled by womanright, that is, by marriage with the hereditary owner of the land. This ownership of the land descended through Eve from mother to daughter by ultimogeniture, that is, to the youngest, not the eldest, daughter of the line. Thus, David ruled over a unified Israel through his marriages to the heiresses of the twelve tribes. Simon points out a similar tradition in Egypt where the pharoah marries his sister, and in Crete, Cyprus, Greece, and Rome.

Simon explains to the incredulous Antipater that no king has a true title to rule in Israel unless he is married to the Heiress of Michal, King David's wife. The female line of Michal was absorbed through marriage, however, into the House of Eli, whose members were thereafter considered the Heirs of David. This creates a political problem.

The House of Eli hates Herod. For this reason, and for other more personal political considerations, Simon has never revealed to Herod that he could stabilize his somewhat shaky leadership over the people of Israel by marrying Miriam (Mary), now a temple virgin. As an insurance against the unstable wrath of Herod, who was already ravaged by cancer, and to assure the succession of the more-just Antipater rather than his malicious half-brothers, Simon contracts a secret marriage between Antipater and Mary. Jesus is conceived of this union.

In order to avoid suspicion and danger to the unborn child and his mother (for Herod has already murdered some of his heirs), Simon then betroths Mary to Joseph, a pious and generous old man. A tiny percentage of the marriage debt to the high priest, which completes the legal marriage contract, is withheld.

Herod hears rumors of a possible heir to the throne and plans to massacre all young male children who might be considered the heirs of David. Joseph, whose own family is already grown and independent, undertakes the protection of the young mother and her baby, and flees with them into Egypt. When Herod's devious plotting brings about the violent death of Antipater, Joseph sends the remainder of the marriage debt to Simon from Egypt and becomes Mary's legal husband. Thus closes the first section of the novel.

Part Two recounts Jesus' preparation for his ministry, including a temporary sojourn with the strict religious order of the Essenes, the so-called temptation by the devil (a forty-day fast and ritual trial presided over by the now-aged Simon, acting ceremonially as the devil's advocate), his baptism by John the Baptist, and his marriage to another heiress of Michal, who is Mary, the sister of Martha and Lazarus.

The latter event, one of the most surprising deviations from gospel accounts, fulfills the requirement already explained, which is that the true king of Israel becomes legitimate only through marriage to the female heir to the land. The wife, Mary, also represents the second person of the ancient pagan Triple Goddess, mother, bride, and layer-out. But Jesus refuses to consummate the marriage, thus repudiating the bondage of the senses.

This symbolic declaration of war against the Female (against nature itself perhaps) results in a more intellectual duel with the third Mary, who plays the role of layer-out (in death) to man. She is represented by the Queen of the Harlots, an old crone called Mary the Hairdresser. This is the biblical Mary Magdalene, from whom Jesus exorcised seven devils. The exorcism in the novel is not strikingly different from the biblical one, except that it follows an evenly matched debate between Mary the Hairdresser and Jesus about the true meaning of certain sacred relics.

One recognizes here the voice of comparative mythologist Graves, demonstrating that many an ancient tableau graven on ritual icons can be interpreted as demonstrating either Old Testament, biblical stories or the more ancient mythology of the Great Goddess. According to Graves, the misinterpretation of religious icons from an older culture often accounts for changes in the structure of myths. In this case, Jesus interprets the pictures as scenes from the Old Testament. Mary the Hairdresser interprets them as the more ancient myth of Mother Eve bearing twin sons, who contend with each other for the love of the Second Eve, until sacrificed by the Third Eve.

Jesus cannot by persuasion convert Mary the Hairdresser from her devotion to the pagan fertility goddess. It is then, as a last resort, he exorcises her seven deadly sins by a feat of magic. Yet, though Jesus wins temporarily this contest, Mary the Hairdresser is not finally beaten, for her last words to Jesus are: "Nevertheless, Lord, the end is not yet, and when the Mother summons me to my duty, I will not fail her." This is foreboding, indeed, for at the foot of the cross will be Mary the Mother, Mary the Bride, and Mary the Layer-out.

Part Three of *King Jesus* deals with the series of events that lead to Jesus' crucifixion. Although Jesus refuses to consummate the marriage, an obligation he owes to the second Mary under Jewish law, he cannot so easily evade the ritual death that the Goddess as Crone always exacts of her chosen hero.

The beginning of the end involves his raising Lazarus, his wife's brother, from the dead. Although Mary has sent messages repeatedly to Jesus, begging him to come home and cure the failing Lazarus, Jesus tarries until the man is four days in the tomb. When Jesus finally arrives, Mary is understandably bitter. She demands that Jesus either give her a child, which is her right under the Hebrew law, or bring her beloved brother back by saying the forbidden secret name of God.

This magical rite is within Jesus' capabilities, but one always owes God a life to replace the life given back. In the legendary past, the wonder workers who used this means to resurrect the dead had generously forfeited other people's lives for the purpose. Jesus, of course, cannot willingly cause another person's death. He realizes then that he can only give himself as substitute. Thus Lazarus returns from the dead, but Jesus knows that he has been defeated in his dream of conquering death for all time and ruling the prophesied thousand years of peace before the day of judgment.

From this point, Jesus' behavior subtly changes. He starts drinking and feasting with his disciples. He unaccountably curses the fig tree.[1] When he is next in the temple, he wrathfully overturns the moneychangers' tables and casts out the peddlers of sacrificial animals. (How many moral activists have been thankful for this single display of righteous indignation and violent action!)

But Jesus' most uncharacteristic action, according to this account, is the symbolic eucharist at the Passover feast, called by Christians the Last Supper. When Jesus says of the bread he passes to his disciples "Take, eat; this is my body," and of the wine, "This is my blood," he is deliberately imitating pagan sacrificial rites. Graves says that such a ritual would be considered blasphemous to contemporary Jews. To be sure, Graves is not the first to note that the act of symbolically consuming the body and blood of a human or divine sacrifice predates Christianity in literally cannibalistic pagan ritual. In fact, Judas, the most maligned man in the Christian tradition, asks himself in horror: "What is this? Are we to eat abominable food at our God's own Feast, as the Greeks eat the body and drink the blood of their god in the Mysteries?"

The reference here is probably to the Dionysian Mysteries, for Dionysus was a dying and reviving god closely associated with the Triple Moon-Goddess. Graves says in *The Greek Myths*: "Dionysus began as a type of sacred-king whom the goddess ritually killed with a thunderbolt in the seventh month from the winter solstice, and whom her priestesses devoured."

Graves interprets this "idolatrous eucharist" as indicative of a radical change of role by Jesus. Realizing that he must die as a forfeit for Lazarus, he exchanges the triumphant Son of David messianic role for the scapegoat role of the Suffering Servant:

He had combined in himself Zechariah's prophecy of the Worth-less Shepherd and Isaiah's prophecy of the Suffering Servant—the Marred Man, the Man of Sorrows, who would go to his death as a willing sacrifice and be numbered among the sinners. To be numbered among the sinners is to commit sin, and the Man of Sorrows must sin grievously in order to take the iniquity of all the people upon him: it was the very consciousness of grievous sin that would make him a Man of Sorrows.

Zechariah's prophecy required the Worthless Shep-herd to be a false prophet, so that one very close to him in love will accuse him, "You have spoken lies in the name of Jehovah—you shall not live!" and kill him with a sword. Jesus' attempt to recreate this role leads him to say to his disciples, "One of you twelve shall kill me!"

Thus we come to the last of four major reinterpreta-tions of scripture. Jesus has been presented as fathered by Prince Antipater, married to the second Mary, and reli-giously compromised by a forbidden eucharistic ceremony. Now the despised Judas becomes a pathetic sacrifice, trying first to forestall Jesus' suicidal intent to be assassinated like the Worthless Shepherd, then trying to ransom his master's life with his own death.

Judas is the unlucky person whom Jesus orders to buy a sword and play the righteous assassin of the Worthless Shepherd. Judas is in a quandary, for he knows he cannot do this act. Yet, if he refuses, Jesus may simply convince a more obedient disciple. At last, Judas and Nicodemon con-trive a plot to protect Jesus from following his plan. Judas will arrange for Jesus to be arrested by the Romans, who will surely not kill him, since Jesus has never preached revolu-tion. Judas considers this protective custody.

What Judas did not foresee was that Jesus, who could outtalk the most learned debaters in the temple, would simply refuse any defense and allow himself to be railroaded into a death penalty. Indeed, Pontius Pilate, who had been informed of Jesus' probable lineage, offers privately to present Jesus' claim to kingship to the Roman emperor. But Jesus spurns the offer of a temporal kingdom supported by Romans. When Judas learns that Jesus is sentenced to be crucified, he hangs himself in a futile attempt to ransom with his life and soul the life of Jesus, in accordance with the ancient law of a life for a life. Though Jesus felt he was bound by this law for raising Lazarus, Judas' death, obviously, does not prevent Jesus' crucifixion.

Ironically, the man who sought to overturn the dominion of the female, which in one sense means supplanting the natural order with its alternating birth and death, with a supernatural, spiritual order, ends by reenacting the primitive ritual of the sacrificial king. Yet, when Jesus struggles up the hill of Golgotha to his crucifixion, it is women who attend him. "The news of Jesus's arrest had spread rapidly through the City, and though few of his male supporters dared join the procession, Joanna and Susanna were there, and Mary, Jesus's mother, leaning on the arm of Shelom the midwife; and Mary his queen, with her sister Martha, and their grandmother Mary wife of Cleopas; and Mary the Hairdresser, with a party of Rechabite women." And Mary the Hairdresser, once queen of harlots, says to Shelom, "His fault was this: that he tried to force the hour of doom by declaring war upon the Female. But the Female abides and cannot be hastened."

Moreover, his crucifixion carries implications of primitive sacrificial rites. "Anciently, it seems," comments the narrator, who is a Roman of the first century A.D., "in every country around the Mediterranean Sea, crucifixion was a fate reserved for the annual Sacred King. . . . In every case the Sacred King is regarded as a sacrifice made on behalf of the tribe to its Goddess Mother." Thus, instead of instituting with his death what Paul was to call the "new dispensation" for spiritual salvation, Jesus reenacts the ancient ritual of the dying and reviving god who represents the waning and waxing year and assures the fecundity of nature. The narrator further explains that death by crucifixion was once believed to be a magical means of assuring immortality. Both crucifixion and hanging were involved in ancient tree cults. For that very reason, perhaps, the Jews of Jesus' time, who sought to divorce themselves from all taint of pagan worship, considered both ways of "hanging on the tree" as extinguishing the soul as well as the body.

Much of Graves's lore on tree cults undoubtedly stems from James Frazer's monumental study on myth and religion. For an illuminating discussion of the influence on Graves of Frazer's *The Golden Bough*, consult John B. Vickery's book *Robert Graves and the White Goddess*. Vickery says:

Frazer explodes the idea of the historical purity of Christianity by showing how much it derives from pagan religions that center on a dying and reviving god. In his discussion of the crucifixion of Christ he also provides Graves with a model for reinterpreting the event in terms that square with known rituals as well as with the demands for historical and documentary consistency. The reasons for Jesus' crucifixion adduced by Frazer and Graves are startlingly at odds with the traditional view; they are centered in rituals observed for the dying and reviving god of still earlier times. Frazer suggests Jesus was cast in the role of Haman in the Jewish festival of Purim, which in turn derived from the Babylonian festival of the Sacaea, both of which were Saturnalia involving a mock king and his ritual death.[2] Graves does substantially the same thing, though he compounds the irony by stressing the orthodoxy of Jesus' Jewry while underscoring that his death takes the form of a ritual sacrifice to the heathen goddess he had opposed.[3]

The division of the novel into three parts, Jesus' nativity, his ministry and marriage, and his death also carries mythical associations. The Triple Goddess, man's mother, bride, and layer-out, defines the major divisions of a man's life as birth, marriage, and death. Mary the Hairdresser plays the part of the Crone, who lays out Jesus' body in the tomb. After Jesus rises from the tomb, he is last seen by his disciples in the company of three women: Mary his mother, Mary his wife, and an unnamed, tall, veiled woman. The ending is deliberately shrouded in mystery. The reader does not know whether Jesus simply survived crucifixion, as Graves and certain other writers have suggested elsewhere, or whether he rose supernaturally from the dead. The implication of the trio of women is that Jesus did, indeed, attain immortality as the Sacred King, but in different terms from those he himself taught.

Thus, Graves has created a new myth about Jesus—a myth in many ways quite as fascinating as the accepted Christian version. He has explained in more or less rational terms some of the miracles, retained others, and created some supernatural elements which the Bible does not contain. Graves lends some credence to such an interpretation by using a first century narrator who is neither Jewish nor Christian. As a pagan, he believes in the supernatural but looks upon the Jewish efforts to stamp out all remnants of the powerful fertility cults as probably misguided. One cannot cancel out nature, the Great Mother.

Graves and Joshua Podro, who collaborated on *The Nazarene Gospel Restored*, wrote in *Jesus in Rome*, an epilogue to that volume:

Jesus, like his fellow Apocalyptics, expected the present world to end during his lifetime in a series of catastrophes known as the 'Pangs of the Messiah.' The Kingdom of Heaven, which would then be inaugurated and last for a thousand years, with Jerusalem for its capital, was to be a heaven on earth, peopled partly by risen saints, partly by a few living saints who would not die until the world ended.

Do not assume, however, that the novel *King Jesus* corresponds to the historical Jesus which Graves and Podro tried to recapture in *The Nazarene Gospel Restored*. Some of the unorthodox ideas in the novel receive some discussion in *The Nazarene Gospel Restored*, as derived from ancient legends, but are often rejected by the writers—

sometimes for equally unorthodox views. The identity of Jesus's mother is a case in point. In *The Nazarene Gospel Restored*, the authors point out that a view "apparently held by a section of first-century Gentile Christians" was that the Messiah was a lost royal heir—that is, legitimately fathered on Mary by Antipater, the eldest son of King Herod. Antipater's arrest and trial would account for Mary's hurried flight to Elizabeth and the strange circumstances of her subsequent marriage, which suggest an effort at concealment from Herod's agents. Herod's Massacre of the Innocents then makes sense if he had heard rumors of a grandson. Herod had Messianic pretensions of his own.

Having advanced this theory, used fictionally by Graves in *King Jesus*, the authors admit that it does not stand up well under scrutiny. John the Baptist, it was reasoned in *The Nazarene Gospel Restored*, would not have anointed a Roman citizen, "a scion of the usurping and pagan House of Herod; nor is the Massacre of Bethlehem recorded in any other document, either non-Jewish or Jewish."

Graves and Podro, as a matter of fact, account for the virgin birth in altogether different terms. They say that when John the Baptist conducted a coronation of Jesus as King of the Jews, Jesus was ritually reborn, that is, adopted by Mary, one of the temple virgins. This established him symbolically as Son of God. Graves chose not to use this version of the story in the novel, though he apparently derived the name Mary the Hairdresser (presumably the biblical Mary Magdalene) from the name he found in the Talmud for the Levite temple virgin. Graves and Podro say in *Jesus in Rome:*

From certain signs, John [the Baptist] recognized Jesus as the prophesied King of Israel who would lead his people back to God; and a few days later crowned him secretly with ancient ceremony (see *N.G.R.*, VIII). Since the Messiah, in fulfillment of the prophecies found in *The Testament of the Twelve Patriarchs*—a book accepted by these Apocalyptics—was to be born of David, yet also to be a priest of the House of Aaron, John the Baptist apparently arranged for Jesus's ritual adoption by a young Levite relative of his own (Luke: 26–56). She was named Mary M'gaddla, 'the Braider' (Talmud: Sanhedrin, 67a), because she worked with other Levite girls on the annual Veil of the Temple (Protoevangelium 10–11). This, we believe, explains the account of the Virgin Birth, his mother being and remaining a virgin, and also the two irreconcilable genealogies given him in *Matthew* i and *Luke* iii—one being his Levite pedigree, which has been clumsily altered by Christian editors into a Davidic one.

Although the marriage of Jesus is mentioned as a strong possibility in *The Nazarene Gospel Restored*, considering the ancient principle of matrilinear descent, the topic is not rigorously pursued. One suspects that there was little evidence to support this novel idea. For literary purposes, however, it supported a basic thematic concern of the novel: that is, Jesus' ambiguous position in relation to women. The fact that sexual intercourse made a man ritually unclean for three days accounts at least partially for Jesus' asceticism and his recommending celibacy to his disciples. [4] The imminent coming of the Kingdom of Heaven suggested that they should be in constant readiness to enter that Kingdom.

Even the curious emphasis on the Female as Jesus's adversary has a precedent in ancient documents. A quotation from Clement of Alexandria precedes the novel:

When in *The Gospel according to the Egyptians*, Shelom asked the Lord: "How long shall death prevail?" He answered: "So long as you women bear children. . . ." And when she asked again: "I have done well then in not bearing children?" He answered: "Eat every plant but that which is bitter. . . ." And when she inquired at what time the things concerning which she had questioned Him should be known, He answered: "When you women have trampled on the garment of shame and when the two become one, and when the male with the female is neither male nor female. . . ." And the Saviour said in the same Gospel: "I have come to destroy the works of the Female." [5]

Jesus's claim to heroic stature in this story seems to me to rest upon his metaphysical revolt, on behalf of all men, against inevitable sin and death. If the Great Goddess seems to enforce her ancient pattern upon Jesus, yet she is subtly changed by him also. With Jesus's exorcism of the devils from Mary the Hairdresser, her high priestess, a new, more benevolent nature seems possible. The bonds of matter, the bonds of the senses to physical nature, seem loosened. Perhaps transcendence is possible, as in Aeschylus's *Oresteia*, where the terrible, blood-stained Furies that pursue Orestes, the matricide, are transformed into the Eumenides, the Benevolent Ones. Perhaps the tragic hero does indeed make the gods more just.

10

Satirical Writings

On those few occasions when Graves has deserted mythological or historical themes in novels, the result is a strange, acrid, improbable story, lucidly told, but somehow disquieting. He and Laura Riding, writing under the pseudonym of Barbara Rich, collaborated on a fanciful novel called *No Decency Left*. It is a satirical potpourri of events, suggesting such discordant elements as the rise of dictators, the man in the iron mask, the miraculous feeding of the multitude in the Bible, and comic-opera romance.

The action occurs in one day, the twenty-first birthday of Barbara Rich. Barbara is an orphan who has supported herself since age fourteen, now working in a department store. She lives in a shabby rooming house in a kingdom called Lyonesse, probably intended as a Lilliputian version of Britain.

Barbara decides that on this special day she is going to get everything she wants—and she does. She crashes high society, becomes incredibly rich, marries the heir to the throne, feeds a multitude of hungry unemployed by invading the zoo and arranging for the slaughter and cooking on the spot of zoo animals, captures the communists who try to take over the country when the old king dies, and becomes a dictator in her own almost-bloodless revolution.

She is responsible for a number of nasty deaths during the day, however, including her former boyfriend, also a newspaper man she dislikes and tortures for a while, and her husband's twin brother, whose existence is a wellkept state secret. Well, that last wasn't really her fault, but she has the body stashed away for future use in a deep freeze. She tells the king that if he ever tires of her leadership, he can skip out and she will produce his brother's body to cover his escape. She knows she has no permanent need for the king, though she is in love with him at the moment. (The resemblance to the White Goddess is striking!)

This outrageous scenario could be converted into a hilarious Hollywood comedy, but its tone would have to change. No one is lovable here; in fact, everyone is despicable.

At the end of this elaborate coup, when Barbara wakes up in the middle of her wedding night, she has a vision of two gates and two roads. A sign above one, through which all the ordinary people she knows (now her subjects) are thronging, reads "No Moral Courage." They are likened to sheep, and they are crowding into "a dismal suburban lane which wound slowly uphill between tarred fences, and eventually disappeared over a residential skyline." But through the second imposing gate nobody passes but herself.

And from it led slowly underground a shiny black road, ever so wide, and quite empty except for two rows of beacon lights, one on either side, converging gorgeously towards an unguessable End. And she was walking without a tremor down into that fate—alone. And the legend on the vast steel gate said: "No Decency Left."

The message seems to be that people are either uniformly stupid and cowardly or utterly unscrupulous. Is Barbara supposed to be beyond good and evil, though going downhill? (A parody of Nietzsche's Superman, perhaps?) Is she to be admired because she shows how an intelligent person, who is entirely self-centered and honest with herself, could perform virtual miracles?

Why and how is such a book conceived? One can only speculate. If it had been published just a few years later (instead of 1932), one could suggest that it satirizes the blanket powers accorded to Hitler by the Reichstag (1933) or his becoming dictator (1934), and perhaps the famous love affair of King Edward with the commoner, Wallis Simpson, and abdication on her behalf (1936). But unless the authors were clairvoyant, this topical application is accidental.

The Soviet revolution provides the more obvious referent, if any is intended, and certain literary traditions. The twin brother is likened in the novel to the legendary man in the iron mask, supposedly brother to the king. The tragic love between royalty and commoner is a familiar theme of popular romance—given an ironic twist here, since love becomes a secondary project to a person who enjoys sheer power.

One can imagine an irreverent planning session for this novel. Let us suppose that Robert Graves and Laura Riding need some money (as they sometimes did, since their poetry had only a limited audience.) They ask themselves what would sell the best to those millions of frustrated housewives? Cinderella, Laura says contemptuously; but I can't abide that passive little waif who has to be sought out by the handsome prince. Make her a resolute superwoman who can leap over poverty with a single bound, subjugate a prince and everybody else with her beauty and wit, and lead the masses with spontaneous oratory. . . . You have to have an adequate adversary, though, or it's no contest, cautions Robert mildly. Everyone is afraid of the commies these days—we could have a communist takeover, which would threaten to nullify the protagonist's conquest of the handsome prince. . . . OK, says Laura, as long as Cinderella has an even more spectacular takeover from the commies.

Let's put in a sly biblical reference suggesting she is a new messiah—the best you can find in these degenerate times, says Robert. . . . How could we work that, asks Laura, dubiously. . . . Well, aside from the commies, the biggest social horror is unemployment and attendant hunger. Dostoevsky's Grand Inquisitor was right, you know, muses Robert—people will lay their freedom at the feet of whoever provides food. . . . Yes, says Laura, just look at us debasing ourselves to write a popular novel just because we need money. Well, what should Cinderella do, raid a supermarket and pass out forbidden apples and oranges to the poor? . . . No, says Robert, delving deeper into the mythological past, there must be a primitive symbolic feast with fire and sacrificial slaughter. . . . Why, asks Laura, Christ didn't do it that way when he fed the multitude with a few loaves and fishes. . . . How do we know? The distasteful parts of the story have been changed to fit more genteel tastes, mutters Robert crossly. We simply have to slaughter animals. . . . What animals in a city—stray dogs? They wouldn't be very nourishing in depression times. . . . (Which writer suggested giraffe, bison, bear, and suckling elephant, I wonder, to serve for loaves and fishes?)

The view of the human animal, male or female, as vicious, with superior cleverness and ingenuity the mark of the female, also dominates Graves's novel *The Antigua Stamp* (*Antigua, Penny, Puce,* 1936). The everlasting battle of the sexes is dramatized here as sibling rivalry that is never outgrown. The brother is an amateur philatelist who makes the mistake of admitting to his sister, in childhood, that she may claim half ownership in his stamp collection. She makes a few insignificant additions to "their" stampbook, to make good the bond. Brother and sister really can't stand each other, however, and a long-standing, sour feud ends, when they are adults (in age, at least), in her insisting that the stamps be divided equally between them. The final big hassle is over the ownership of the Antigua Stamp, which proves to be one of the most valuable in the world, because all the rest of that printing was lost in a shipwreck. Well, of course, the female wins because she is vastly more clever and conniving than her brother. But they are both thoroughly beastly. Even so, the tone is lighter and more playful than *No Decency Left*. Deliberate potboilers, both, no doubt, and they make entertaining reading. Yet, total contempt for human beings (including readers of potboilers, I suspect) need earn no particular accolades. Perhaps we should call it "Swiftian."

There is a distinct similarity in tone to the closing barbs of Graves's essay "Mrs. Fisher, or the Future of Humour." This acid passage from that essay, published in *Occupation: Writer*, is obviously in the spirit of "The Modest Proposal," though too bludgeoning to match Swift's rapier style.[1]

Realistic humour has great capabilities in the hands of those with energy enough to add more wheels and cranks and cylinders to the insensate machinery of civilization, to make it function still more crankily. Perhaps Mrs. Fisher is the woman to organize the task; certainly no man would ever have the deadly thoroughness needed to carry it through. She will, I believe, first reveal herself in a series of embarrassing gifts to civilization; cheap and unsafe family aeroplanes, synthetic food at a nominal cost, minute but powerful pocket wireless sets that can be pinned on a coat lapel, a perfectly simple, fool-proof contraceptive that is at the same time an effective oestrific, a new humanitarian religion based on the left-handed Sakta cult, an undetectable poison (of which she alone has the antidote) with an unrestricted sale at all grocers' shops, and an infallible system of prognosticating the winners of horse and dog races. After that she will proclaim herself Dictator and take control of the entire State, which will also be the much-heralded World State, and ride in a coach drawn by six white asses and an ostrich, and set up a nude statue of herself two miles high at Braintree, Essex, and marry M. Judy, the French President, in a little synagogue in Marrakesh, compelling him to take her name and sign the register as Mr. Fisher—after which she will sacramentally eat him.

In 1930, Graves published an accumulation of odd pieces in *But It Still Goes On*—a further cleaning out of his files, so to speak, begun with *Goodbye to All That*. The collection includes some further remarks on his autobiography, an excellent short story called "The Shout" (see next chapter), portions of a diary called "A Journal of

Curiosities," a satirical biography of God called "Alpha and
Omega of the Autobiography of Baal," and an atrociously
bad-tempered play called "But It Still Goes On."

Graves had long renounced the Christianity of his
childhood, so the pseudo-autobiography of Baal (one of
God's aliases) displays considerable cynicism along with
some half-serious thought about the origins of religion. In
the Alpha portion, for instance, God explains that he began
as a vividly felt but impossible to be expressed difference
between things that seem practically similar. More specifically, between the way that men make or do things and the
way that things make themselves or "happen." So his first
name meant "Why?" Since cause and effect hadn't been
thought of yet, the only answer to "Why?" was "Why!"

Sects like the Mormons and Christian Scientists rate
some satirical observations. Catholicism is treated with tol-
erant condescension as appealing to the immature. "When
I said 'Suffer the little children to come unto me, for of such
is the kingdom of Heaven,' I gave the final justification of
the Church of Rome."

All little children, all sheep without a shepherd, all those pure in
heart because unstable in mind, all the charming, the fanciful, the
passionate, the devoted, the rebellious, the repentant, all those
who find it impossible to live happily with no more than a sense of
expediency or a fear of legal consequences to restrain their impulses, all baffled poets, all natural liers and dissemblers, all those
who are chilled by my inhuman aspect as Reason, all those who
have shame, all, all are the natural members of this spiritual
kindergarten. . . .

Nevertheless, this facetious document is not nearly so
cynical and vindictive as the play "But It Still Goes On,"
which seems to be a projection upon the whole world of
Graves's overwhelming disgust. Dick, Graves's spokesman,
assures us that the whole bottom has dropped out of the
world—I presume that means whatever provided meaning
or value is irrevocably gone. The action of the play sym-
bolizes the utterly hopeless condition of society. George

Stade has provided an admirably succinct precis of the action:

David, a homosexual, marries Dorothy, sister to Dick whom David loves; and Charlotte, a lesbian, would have married Dick because she loves Dorothy, but out of an objectless spite marries Cecil, Dick's and Dorothy's father, who is nevertheless a rival of Dick's for Elizabetta, who is having an affair with Pritchard, who is a poet, as are his rivals, Dick and Cecil. Dorothy, learning of David's preference for men, shoots him. Charlotte, still spiteful, but now pregnant as well, claiming (dishonestly) that Dick has seduced her, maliciously commits suicide by throwing herself over a banister. Once the two queers are out of the way, the others, led by Dick, torment Cecil, representative of a vestigially prestigious older generation, into shooting himself. Remorseless over the dead body, they tell the police that he had confessed to murdering David. [2]

Considering that this play came out the year after Graves's wife Nancy left him, and Laura Riding jumped from an upper window because a man she fancied preferred Nancy, and Graves chose to stick with Laura—perhaps the kindest thing to do is simply look the other way and forgive the man his cry of agony. Graves admitted in the introduction to *Occupation: Writer* that it was "a tactful reshuffling of actual events and situations in which I had been more or less closely concerned." Though the play may have been therapeutic for Graves, I doubt that it will be so for readers.

The mental and emotional sickness from which the play arises was probably not just a reaction to domestic crisis, however, though that crisis may have suggested ways of dramatizing his feeling in concrete images. It expresses a general malaise, by no means confined to Graves, resulting from the experiences of World War I. Daniel Hoffman quotes Edwin Muir in a passage that, as Hoffman points out, seems particularly relevant to Graves. Muir is discussing the situation for poets in 1926:

The poet is not concerned because ideals do not correspond to realities (a great source of pessimistic poetry); he is hardly concerned with ideals at all. His bewilderment springs from something far more complex: the feeling that reality itself has broken down, that even the simple emotions, the instinctive reactions, are disoriented and lead us astray.[3]

Graves wrote two long essays in this gloomy period. One, which has already been quoted in this chapter, is "Mrs. Fisher, or the Future of Humour." Only occasionally can the reader even smile. "'Lars Porsena,' or the Future of Swearing and Improper Language," also in *Occupation: Writer*, is more entertaining. It regrets the decline of swearing in England, assuming, however, that future disasters may reactivate a lost art. It considers class distinctions in the seriousness of certain oaths. Bastardy is a serious charge in the lower classes, for instance, but in the upper classes "natural sons" are tolerated very comfortably, may win high offices, etc. He has some interesting things to say about grammatical constructions: "bloody," for instance, "may be used verbally, adjectivally, adverbially, as an interjection, or as an enclitic, in such interruptive forms as 'of bloody course' and 'abso-bloody-lutely.'" He brings up the many word taboos regarding sex and other bodily functions, dwelling upon the absurd euphemisms substituted for them. Finally, he imagines a researcher of the future trying to fathom the clues to an unrecorded language:

Some historian of the future will discuss the social taboos of the nineteenth and twentieth centuries in a fourteen-volume life work. He will postulate the existence of an enormous secret language of bawdry and an immense oral literature of obscene stories and rhymes known in various degrees of initiation, to every man and woman in the country, yet never consigned to writing or openly admitted as existing. His contemporaries will dismiss the theory as fantastic. . . .

One can, indeed, imagine a thirtieth century incarnation of Robert Graves ferreting out the secret language of obscenity (which is not today, however, quite so unrecorded) and defending his theories against the combined scorn of the academic establishment. Critical reaction would be a variation, perhaps, of Graves's experience with *The White Goddess, King Jesus,* and *The Nazarene Gospel Restored.* But Graves would enjoy every minute of it.

At least two of Graves's translations might appropriately be grouped with satirical works. Few will quarrel with this placement for the delightful *The Golden Ass.* Readers may wince at the inclusion of Homer's Iliad, but Graves chooses to emphasize its satiric elements.

Graves's lucid translation from ornate Latin into faultless English prose of Lucius Apuleius' *The Transformation of Lucius,* otherwise known as *The Golden Ass,* preserves both its ironic, sometimes bawdy, humor and its serious moral import.[4] For all its spicy jests and folktales, *The Golden Ass* is a religious novel. Christians have seldom taken seriously, perhaps, its celebration of the variously named goddess of nature, partly because the Judeo-Christian tradition has so vigorously excluded all laughter and recognition of the ridiculous from the oppressive consciousness of sin. Jehovah's punishments for sin bring no rueful smiles to anyone's lips. But the more naturalistic tradition of Greece and Rome sometimes reveals sin as folly, which may produce a ludicrous penalty of its own.

What more ludicrous fate to a rash young man than to be transformed unexpectedly into an ass? "In Apuleius's day," explains Graves in the introduction, "the ass typified lust, cruelty and wickedness." Originally, the ass was sacred to the Egyptian god Set, who murdered Osiris, husband to goddess queen Isis. It was thus the most hated beast to great Isis, the primary name of the nature goddess who eventually succours the miserable Lucius, transforms him again into a man, and initiates him into her own mysteries. He is henceforth a priest of Isis.

Though it may seem presumptuous to Christians, Graves compares the religious import of the tale to the confessions of Augustine, Apuleius' fellow countryman. They are both stories of folly, repentence, and conversion.

The author of *The Golden Ass* was a priest of Isis and Osiris, possibly after a somewhat dissolute youth, and also a

poet and a historian. He was born in a Roman colony in
Morocco, early in the second century A.D., attended
Carthage University, and later went to Athens to study
Platonic philosophy. In Corinth, Apuleius was accused of
black magic and defended himself with an amusing speech,
which still survives as A *Discourse on Magic.*

Though acquitted of the charge, this accusation was
enough to make some Christians assume the miraculous
events in *The Golden Ass* were literal truth. As Graves
points out: "Evidently St. Augustine and his credulous contemporaries had not read Lucius of Patra's popular novel
The Ass, now lost, or Lucian of Samosata's *Lucius, or the
Ass,* still extant, which is based on it; otherwise, they would
have realized that Apuleius had borrowed the plot of *The
Transformations* from one or other of these two sources."
Thus, Apuleius did not invent the stories but undoubtedly
improved upon the originals.

Apuleius constantly uses a device now known on the variety stage
as the 'double take.' The audience applauds, but finds that it has
applauded too soon; the real point, either funnier or more macabre
than anyone expected, was yet to come. The brilliance of his show-
manship suggests that he turned professional story-teller during his
wanderings in Greece, using Lucius of Patra's *Ass* as his stock-
piece—he felt its relevance to his case and Lucius happened to be
his own name—and stringing a number of popular stories to it.

Lucius's folly, which brings on the misery of transformation into an ass that is beaten, over-worked, and driven
from one master to another in constant fear for his life, is
this: though a nobleman, he engages in a frivolous love
affair with a girl enslaved by a known witch. His express
purpose is to induce the slave to betray her mistress's secrets
of black magic. When the witch transforms herself into a
bird, Lucius covets this novel experience. He gets the slave
to steal some of the magic ointment that the witch used on
her body. The girl makes an unfortunate mistake, however,
and steals the wrong ointment. Poor Lucius is transformed
into the most ignominious of beast shapes—an ass. Before

the girl can get the antidote to this spell, the ass is stolen by thieves. Thereby, as the saying goes, hangs a tale.

Both Christians and educated pagans of this period agreed that black magic was an inappropriate pursuit for the honorable man. In his introduction, Graves writes:

Recent researches into the history of witchcraft show that Apuleius had a first-hand knowledge of the subject. The Thessalian witches preserved the pre-Aryan tradition of a 'left-hand', or destructive, magic performed in honour of the Triple Moon-goddess in her character of Hecate; the 'right-hand,' or beneficient, magic performed in honour of the same Goddess being now concentrated in the pure mysteries of Isis and Demeter. It must be remembered that in St. Augustine's day the sovereignty of the indivisible male Trinity had not yet been encroached upon by Mariolatry, and Apuleius's splendid address to Isis could not therefore be read with indulgence as an anticipation of the *Liturgy of the Blessed Virgin* with which it has much in common. Apuleius did not deny the power of the left-hand cult, any more than the Christians denied the power of the Devil: but he knew that honourable men like himself ought to leave it alone and that if they kept strictly to the right-hand cult, the devotees of the left-hand could have no power over them.

The account is filled with folk stories, which the ass, who retains his human intelligence, overhears in his painful journey. The best known elaboration of primitive folk tale is the Cupid and Psyche story. As Graves explains, ". . . taking hints from passages in Plato's *Phaedo* and *Republic* he turned it into a neat philosophical allegory of the progress of the rational soul toward intellectual love. This feat won him the approval even of the better sort of Christians, including Synnesius the early fifth-century Bishop of Ptolemais. . . ."

Many of the stories are more akin to medieval French fabliaux, like that immortalized in Chaucer's "Miller's Tale"—bawdy tales of deceit and adultery. Other stories include elements of barbaric cruelty, suggesting that everyday life in those times was often hazardous because of ruthless, organized banditry. The stories provide insight into the different levels of society, local customs (such as the Festival

of Laughter), popular forms of entertainment—all in so
readable a style that modern audiences can enjoy it more
readily than many a modern novel.

Graves has made an equally readable translation of
Homer's Iliad into contemporary prose and poetry. The
poetic interludes in the otherwise prose narrative are short,
often prayers to the gods, or some of the more notable
Homeric similes or dramatic situations. No attempt is made
to reproduce the original dactylic hexameter lines. Graves
has converted them into modern verse forms, often qua-
trains or sextets or series of rhymed couplets, varying from
two to five metric feet to the line. Thus the style is quite
different from the Richmond Lattimore translation, perhaps
the most widely used Homeric text in academia. Here is
Lattimore's translation of Agamemnon's prayer to Zeus for
victory in Book Two:

> 'Zeus, exalted and mightiest, sky-dwelling in the dark mist:
> let not the sun go down and disappear into darkness
> until I have buried headlong the castle of Priam
> blazing, and lit the castle gates with the flame's destruction;
> not till I have broken at the chest the tunic of Hektor
> torn with the bronze blade, and let many companions about
>   him
> go down headlong into the dust, teeth gripping the ground
>   soil.' "

Here is Graves's version of that prayer:

> 'O Zeus, greatest of gods
>   In Heaven residing,
> With unabated power
>   The storm cloud riding:

> 'Let not this sun go down,
>   Nor darkness flout me,
> Till I and these seven kings
>   Here grouped about me

> 'Have fired the many-doored
>   Dwelling of Priam,

> That not one wall may stand
>> So tall as I am;
>
> 'Till swords have rent the bright
> Tunic of Hector,
> And ringed him round with dead—
>> Troy's doomed protector.'

Graves's poetry seems unnecessarily simplistic in style. He claims to reactivate, though in different terms, the qualities of rhythm and rhyme that were important to the oral delivery of professional bards. Graves complains in the introduction, "Translations are made for the general, non-Classical public, yet their authors seldom consider what will be immediately intelligible, and therefore readable, and what will not." Graves points out that the most accurate rendering does not necessarily do justice to Homer. In illustration he uses a passage by Lattimore from Book Six, beginning,

> Bellerophontes went to Lykia in the blameless
>> convoy
> of the gods; when he came to the running stream
>> of Xanthus, and Lykia,
> the lord of wide Lykia tendered him full-hearted
>> honour. . . .

Graves begins this passage thus: "The Olympians brought Bellerophon safe to the mouth of Lycian River Xanthus, where Iobates received him splendidly. . . ."

Graves mentions that in translating *The Golden Ass*, he deliberately used a "staid but simple" English prose to convey the irony implied in Apuleius's absurdly ornate Latin, but he could not do the same with Homer. Much of the Iliad is very suitably translated into prose, but there are lyrical passages and dramatic occasions that call for poetry. "A solemn prayer, a divine message, a dirge, or a country song disguised as a simile—they sound all wrong when turned into English prose: just as wrong as when muster-rolls and long, detailed accounts of cooking a meal or harnessing a mule are kept in verse."

The delightful illustrations done by Ronald Searle for the hardback edition add immeasurably to the effect of Graves's ironic approach to the "message" of the Iliad. These caricatures of gods and men undoubtedly accentuate the long-recognized "Homeric laughter" that underlies much of the action, particularly the less-than-helpful interference of the gods. Who can resist an obese Zeus beating his chest, hair and beard flying wildly, one fist shaking a bundle of lightning, as he orates: "At my strong hands that God shall earn egregious punishment. . . ." Hera, his long-suffering wife, looks on behind him with an expression of unutterable boredom. Or the amply proportioned, naked Aphrodite, goddess of love and beauty, snatching up the callow youth, her darling Paris, as a formidable Menelaus bears down on him like a juggernaut. Nonetheless, Graves and Searle probably overstate the case for satiric intent in Homer.

Graves contends that scholars have too often disregarded the entertainment motive in Homer. He points out the numerous satiric touches directed against both the gods and men (especially the Greek heroes). The Iliad is "tragedy salted with humour." It is comparable not so much to the *Aeneid*, the *Inferno*, or *Paradise Lost*, all most solemn and intellectual, but to Cervantes's *Don Quixote* and Shakespeare's later plays.

The analogy to *Don Quixote* is particularly apt from a modern point of view. Both the Iliad and the Cervantes masterpiece celebrate an outmoded way of life in which human foibles aggravate a human destiny already sufficiently cursed with pain and death. When that which provides meaning and value to human beings conspires with the more destructive elements of nature, the result is so grim as to require the armor of laughter. The famous shield of Achilles, though wrought by Haephastus, the armorer of the gods, is hardly adequate protection. It may indeed be a monstrous delusion.

11

Other Prose

Graves has been involved in so many different kinds of writing projects that any expected grouping leaves out a number of curious documents. He has translated not only Greek and Latin texts, but also German, French, and Spanish—none, I suspect, in purely literal terms. He defends his modern versions as a service to the general public.

Graves claims to dislike the Latin writer Lucan, for instance, yet he spent six months translating his *The Civil Wars* (*Pharsalia*) for modern readers. This concerns the wars between Julius Caesar and Pompey. Graves calls Lucan "the father of yellow journalism," glorying in both sensational brutality and sentimental virtue. These preferences make Lucan peculiarly appropriate for modern audiences, according to Graves. He says in the introduction ". . . like other prodigiously vital writers with hysterical tendencies. . . Lucan exerts a strange fascination on even the reluctant reader; and because, as I have tried to show, he anticipates so many of the literary *genres* dominant today that it would be unfair not to put him in modern dress for the admiration of the great majority whose tastes differ from mine."

In both his translation of Lucan and his rendering of Suetonius's *The Twelve Caesars*, Graves makes no claim for literal translation. He suggests that a literal rendering of Latin into English is almost unreadable. Moreover, he inserts into the texts explanatory material, which, in a literal translation would have to appear in footnotes, for the better comprehension of those unfamiliar with the Roman world. Lucan refers to "wars worse than civil," for instance, without explaining why they are worse. Graves's text reveals the reason: the fact that Julius Caesar and Pompey were relatives.

His most interesting translation from the Spanish is *The Cross and the Sword*, a romantic, historical novel originally named *Enriquillo*, by Manuel de Jesús Galvan. Graves calls this work "the best novel produced by the Indianist movement (i.e., the nineteenth-century literary movement which had the Indian as its chief subject and inspiration, in Spanish America." Galvan was born in Santo Domingo in 1834, ten years before the establishment of the Dominican Republic.

The novel concerns the injustices perpetrated by Spanish settlers of the 16th century upon the Indians on the island of Hispaniola and the subsequent revolt of the Indian leader Enriquillo. Enriquillo led the Indian serfs into the mountains and defied all attempts by the Spanish to capture him and his people for over thirteen years. Eventually his claims to freedom were acknowledged by the Spanish crown and he negotiated an honorable peace. According to this account, Enriquillo maintained throughout a human and defensive war insofar as his attackers allowed him to do so, never giving up the devout Christian ideals he had learned. His cause was always championed by the monk Bartolomé de las Casas, who later became Bishop of Chiapas. Las Casas wrote A *History of the Indies*, which provided much of the historical background for this novel.

Strange to say, Graves has even "translated" English, eliminating what he considers glaring faults in otherwise competent writers. Thus, his temerity at producing *The Real David Copperfield*—Charles Dickens purged of some of his more tasteless sentimentalities. "The root of the modern difficulty with Dickens," says Graves in the foreword to his new improved *Copperfield* "is in his continual readiness to sacrifice straightforwardness in writing to a tradesman-like exploitation of the now extinct Dear Reader."

This exasperation with the way even professional writers misuse language leads us to Graves's book-length treatise on the development and use of English. To be sure, Graves had lectured on language at universities; one such lecture was published in a small volume as *Impenetrability; or, The Proper Habit of English* (1926). In 1943, however, Graves collaborated with Alan Hodge to produce *The Reader over Your Shoulder,* a handbook for writers of English prose. It has two main parts. The first nine chapters explain the historical development of the English language, fashionable styles of the past such as classical and romantic, modern experimentation with language by such writers as E. E. Cummings and James Joyce. Beginning with Chapter Ten, the authors offer a series of twenty-five rhetorical principles for clarity in writing, with illustrations of each.

The first set covers the journalistic requirements—that is, precision about who, what, when, where, how many, how long, etc. Then come statements about syntax, diction, punctuation, problems of ambiguity, needless repetitions or careless omissions. Then matters of logic, transition, consistency of viewpoint. They are all sound, commonsense principles.

The final chapter in Part I is called "The Graces of Prose." The principles deal with such abominations as mixed metaphors or ludicrous combinations of literal and metaphorical language. (A Graham Greene quote: "Kay Rimmer sat with her head in her hands and her eyes on the floor." The authors add, "And her teeth on the mantelpiece?") Other principles concern level of language, affectation, excessively long sentences, obscure references, awkward inversions.

Part II is demonstration of critical analysis using these principles, followed by suitable rewrites that eliminate the difficulties. The examples are from prestigious writers, not student papers: Sir Arthur Eddington's *The Expanding*

Universe, T. S. Eliot's *Elizabethan Essays,* Ernest Hemingway's *For Whom the Bell Tolls,* Sir James Jeans's *The Stars in Their Courses,* F. R. Leavis's *New Bearings in English Poetry,* I. A. Richards's *Principles of Literary Criticism,* Bertrand Russell's *On Education,* A. N. Whitehead's *Science and the Modern World*—and on, and on, for more than two hundred and thirty pages.

Nonetheless, Part II seems more an entertaining game for the authors than a useful demonstration for students of writing. The college students I know who need to use a handbook are seldom ready to improve T. S. Eliot, Bertrand Russell, or I. A. Richards. Writing teachers may indeed ask students to perform tasks of analysis, but the writing blunders in such exercises are much less sophisticated than the ones professional writers usually perpetrate. Students need to recognize the kinds of blunders they themselves make and learn to correct them.

The second part of the book seems to appeal to a somewhat petty satisfaction in exposing the weak moments of otherwise successful writers. As one who has struggled with far more opaque passages by Professor Whitehead than the one offered, I can appreciate his *getting his comeuppance.* (Graves and Hodge would point out that this colloquialism illustrates a violation of the level of language.)

The series of bad examples does emphasize neatly that clear writing requires more constant attention and craft than almost anyone can sustain. But the egotistical implication seems to be that Graves and Hodge are better at writing lucid prose than anyone else of their generation. Perhaps this is a biased judgment from one who has seen too many handbooks and perceived little practical improvement in student writing directly traceable to them. This does not invalidate, however, the excellent writing principles the authors recommend.

In 1927, Graves wrote a biography of his friend T. E. Lawrence, called *Lawrence and the Arabs,* or in America, *Lawrence and the Arabian Adventure.* It is an absorbing account of the Arab revolt and perhaps as effective a characterization as any of the enigmatic Lawrence. Both a scholar and a man of action, Lawrence became a legend in Arabia for his guerrilla warfare, and for inspiring some unity of purpose and cooperation among the fiercely independent tribal chieftains.

He was, nevertheless, a strange case, psychologically speaking, part showman, part recluse, often painfully conscious of divided loyalties. He wore tribal dress on the desert, and often passed for an Arab at night, traveling about to gather information in dangerous territory. Yet, he shaved meticulously every day, so that his blue eyes and clean-shaven face made him instantly recognizable in daylight, his white robes only emphasizing his difference from other men of the desert.

The volume of letters and commentary called *T. E. Lawrence to his Biographers* (1963) shows how closely Lawrence checked the accuracy of the account, and where he insisted on deliberate obscurity or circumlocution. Certain parts of the adventure he declined to divulge, sometimes for personal reasons, apparently, sometimes for political ones.

Lawrence presented a different side of his personality to each of his friends. Lawrence thought of Graves primarily as a poet, and their friendship was based on a mutual interest in literary concerns. To Liddell Hart, whose correspondence with Lawrence occupies the last half of the book of letters, Lawrence deals with military matters. Captain Hart was a military historian.

Hart checked Lawrence's account of the Arab revolt much more closely than Graves did. But Graves says there is little discrepancy between the two accounts, though they are written from different points of view. Lawrence, with his curious impulse to humility or personal concealment, wanted Hart to write a book about the revolt minimizing his own involvement. Apparently that was hardly possible, and Hart's book also became a biography.[1]

Graves drew heavily upon Lawrence's own account of

the revolt, *Seven Pillars of Wisdom*. Graves writes in *T. E. Lawrence to his Biographers*:

I did not intend *Lawrence and the Arabs* as 'literature'. It was a journalistic job, done quickly and, I hoped, inoffensively, and the writing was as subdued and matter-of-fact as I could make it. Two-thirds of the book was a mere condensation of *Seven Pillars* material. As the *Seven Pillars*, however, would not be published during Lawrence's lifetime, nobody complained about this.

Graves's collaboration with Alan Hodge in *The Long Week-End: A Social History of Great Britain 1918–1939* is even more accurately termed a "journalistic job." In fact, it is a journalistic account of what filled the London newspapers between the great wars. It covers such divergent topics as politics, current literary figures, Dr. Stopes's struggles for effective, safe contraceptives, the Loch Ness monster, screen and stage happenings—a chatty, gossipy book on popular culture.

Graves has been a prolific writer of magazine articles and stories, later published in various collections such as ¡*Catatrok*! and *Short Stories*. In spite of the name of the latter and the explanation of the former as "Mostly Stories—Mostly Funny," Graves is not really a short story writer. He has admitted that he has little ability at original invention. He repeats anecdotes told to him by others (especially soldiers), elaborates on experiences of his own, comments on daily life in Majorca, but seldom creates a plot. Sometimes, as in the play "But It Still Goes On," the personal element in the action is quite thinly disguised.

In 1924, however, Graves wrote an excellent short story, "The Shout." He has admitted (in introduction to *Occupation: Writer*) that "Richard in the story is a surrogate for myself: I was still living on the neurasthenic verge of nightmare." Here, however, the autobiographical element is perfectly controlled in an ambiguous tale either of the supernatural or of madness.

The scene is a cricket match at an insane asylum. The

narrator is scoring for the visiting team. The local doctor assures him he will enjoy the local scoresman, named Crossley, who is the most intelligent man in the hospital. He suffers from delusions: one, that he killed three people in Australia, and two, that his soul is split in pieces.

Crossley and the narrator cooperate on the scorekeeping, so Crossley tells a story to while away the time. He tells of a local married couple, Richard and Rachel, who one night both dream of a strange man walking on the sand hills. That morning Richard meets the very man they had seen in their dreams. The man strikes up a conversation, says his name is Charles, and wangles an invitation to dinner. Charles says that he has been living with the Australian aborigines who taught him a terrible shout that killed people or drove men mad.

Richard, not knowing whether to believe the stranger or not, asks to hear the shout. Charles agrees to let him hear a shout i● the first degree, which only terrifies, instead of kills. Charles stays the night and early next morning the two men walk out into the desolate sand hills. Richard is really terrified in anticipation of the experience and covertly stops his ears with wax. Even so, he faints dead away when Charles begins his shout. When he awakens he is lying among the rocks, one of which he picks up. Unaccountably, he begins to think about shoemaking and seems to know all about it. Then he throws away the rock, and he is again himself, a musician.

Richard is quite ill after this episode, but Charles shows up at the house and helps Rachel with the housework. He seems to have a strange hold over her. In fact, Rachel falls in love with Charles, and Richard is ordered to spend the night elsewhere. They have an agreement to honor each other's temporary wayward impulses. Yet Richard is understandably enraged at this invader in his own home.

When he is in town, he learns that his shoemaker had a terrifying experience the very day that Richard had heard

Charles shout. It was as though someone had taken his soul and thrown it away. Richard decides that the rocks at the lonely place where he had fallen must contain the souls of the people who live in the area. He is resolved to find Charles's soul and shatter it.

He takes a hammer and goes to find the stone of Charles's soul. He finds all three, Charles's, Rachel's, and his own. He suddenly has qualms of conscience about killing the soul of a man whom Rachel apparently loves. So instead, he impulsively strikes his own, shattering it in four pieces. Yet, when he gets home he finds that the police have picked up Charles on charges of murder of three people in Australia, and Charles has gone quite mad.

When Crossley finishes the story he says, "Every word of it is true. Crossley's soul was cracked in four pieces and I'm a madman." Meanwhile, a thunderstorm springs up, and Crossley becomes terrified of the thunder. "Oh dear God . . . he'll shout at me again, Crossley will. He'll freeze my marrow." When the doctor runs up to hustle Crossley into the asylum, Crossley threatens to shout and kill them all. As his face becomes distorted, the narrator flees with hands over his ears. A sudden bolt of lightning strikes Crossley and the doctor and kills them instantly.

This story is surely a complex set of dream symbols which work at different levels of interpretation: literary, psychological, and mythical. The insane man perceives himself sometimes as the wronged husband, sometimes as the intruder, his rival—at once the wielder of death and the victim of assault. Even though this story precedes by twenty-four years the publication of *The White Goddess*, Crossley (or Richard) seems analogous to the god of the waxing year who must compete with his blood brother, the god of the waning year, his other self, his "weird," for the love of the woman who accepts each in turn.

The shout—typical of war cries, the purpose of which is to paralyze the enemy with fear—may symbolize, on one level, the experience of war which destroys men's private lives. Richard's combined fascination and dread of hearing the shout, might thus indicate the natural reluctance of the neurotic to assimilate the full significance of his war experience—not to stuff his ears, metaphorically speaking, but to face what can hardly be borne. Yet, the explicit nature of the conflict in the story is not the terror of war at all, but the terror of domestic conflict—the disquieting knowledge that love is tempered with hate and jealousy.

Mythologically speaking, the shout suggests the savage goat-god Pan, whose wild shout caused "panic." Pan was a god of nature and fertility, often representing untamed lust. The shout suggests some untapped, terribly destructive power, perhaps hidden in the subconscious, which threatens to overwhelm stable, civilized life. The lightning that kills Crossley implies a divine judgment on those who nurture such hidden stores of passion and hate.

The fact we learn at the end of the story, that the narrator is staying with the couple, Richard and Rachel, described in Crossley's story, lends a semblance of reality displaced in psychoanalytic terms. The sane person intuits that his own presumably innocuous situation is perhaps loaded with the same possibilities for love and betrayal as Crossley's. The neurotic guilt and fear that haunt the mere possibility of evil makes the violent death of Crossley a personal threat to the beholder. Even if Crossley's story is purely imaginary—the product of an unbalanced mind—the psycho-drama is archetypal and thus "real" perhaps for every man. The narrator must be shaken in whatever confidence he once had in his own sanity, goodness, and self-control.

The notion of souls contained in stones is a more obscure mythical reference, though it has certain natural affinities, perhaps, with stony hearts or broken hearts. It derives possibly from the Greek story of the Deluge—analogous to the Biblical story of Noah. In the Greek myth, Zeus sends the great flood intending to wipe out the whole race of man. Prometheus the Titan warns his son Deucalion, King of Phthia, who builds an ark and thus survives the deluge with his wife Pyrrha. When the water subsides, Deucalion and Pyrrha pray to Zeus that mankind be renewed. In response to their plea, the Goddess Themis appears before them and says, "Shroud your heads, and throw the bones of your mother behind you!" They decide that this cryptic message can only refer to their Mother Earth. Therefore, they throw rocks over their shoulders. The rocks that Pyrrha throws become women, those that Deucalion throws become men. The human race is thus reborn of Mother Earth.

Graves probably uses the idea of souls contained in stones partly because it allows such a concrete image for shattered personality. Richard's choice of spiritual self-destruction rather than spiritual murder—which nevertheless seems to result in his rival's madness—also implies that the two men are aspects of one reality. (Or is the self-sacrificial role the necessary condition for deliverance?) The "I" of the story in effect looks into a psychoanalytic mirror in which the self is seen as containing violently contraditory impulses. Moreover, the sense of guilt this insight brings requires some kind of self-destruction. This impulse is projected upon an imagined avenging Zeus who wields his thunderbolt like the shout that kills. Curiously, the judgment sweeps away the psychoanalyst with his patient. The doctor, therefore, may also represent some function of the narrator, or, one is tempted to guess, a relationship (as that between Graves and Dr. Rivers, the psychoanalyst) that the author must bury with his neurotic past.

On one level, then, this is simply the story of a madman's delusions, but on a psychological level, it is a dream of internal conflict involving love, hate, jealousy, and a perverse impulse to both murder and suicide. Mythically, it may invite contradictory interpretations: an uneasy alternation between good and evil, which induces emotional and moral vertigo, or perhaps a successful purge of the evil self, so that life and love may be redeemed after all.

12

Historical Novels:
on Murder, Milton,
and the Spanish Main

Graves's propensity for historical detective work has resulted
in a varied assortment of novels based on real, rather than
legendary, events, Of these, probably two early ones, *I,
Claudius* and *Count Belisarius*, are the best novels, although the others capture the ambience of a wide variety of
times and places. As a poet who supported himself almost
entirely by his prose, Graves must have been alert for any
historical puzzle that might result in a best seller. Since he
proudly refused to repeat himself (or as he once put it,
produce an *I, Nero* because *I, Claudius* was a winner), he
sometimes chose lesser vehicles for his story-telling talents.
All of them are interesting, however, for their re-creation of
an historical period. The next three chapters deal with these
novels in reverse order to their publication.

They Hanged My Saintly Billy (1957)

This is a minor work about the notorious career and
execution in 1856 of Dr. William Palmer for poisoning his
friend, John Parsons Cook. Palmer's death instigated a
popular protest against capital punishment in Britain. The
dust jacket overestimates the luridness of the contents, as
dust jackets usually do. It quotes Robert Graves's facetious
description of his own product: "My novel is full of sex,
drink, incest, suicides, dope, horse racing, murder, scandalous legal procedure, cross-examinations, inquests and

ends with a good public hanging—attended by 30,000. . . .
Nobody can now call me a specialized writer." One may
safely say this is a potboiler.

Palmer's case was an ambiguous one from the very
beginning. He may well have been innocent of the poisoning for which he was executed, for the evidence was most
circumstantial. In fact, supposed medical experts disagreed
radically about the cause of death. The prosecution's claim
that it was strychnine, but that the poison had been absorbed so that it escaped detection seems a weak argument,
to say the least. However, the case called to mind hitherto
unchallenged instances in Dr. Palmer's past of sudden
deaths that had been remarkably convenient to the doctor.
These vague suspicions combined malevolently with the
fact that he was a gambler and an owner of race horses.
Some claimed that he doped horses that competed with his
own.

Graves employs a clever technique for preserving the
confusion and ambiguity of the case. Most of the novel
consists of personal testimony from persons who had known
Palmer. Thus, each speaker talks from his own biases and
limited contact, some insisting that "he never had it in him
to hurt a fly." Others reveal an incredibly callous schemer
who takes out insurance on his brother's life, knowing him
to be an alcoholic, then arranges that he drink himself to
death. No sure conclusion is ever reached about the justice
of the case. One suspects that Cook died a natural death,
after all, but society could comfortably do without Dr.
Palmer. That, of course, in a more serious book, might
suggest the case of Camus's *Stranger* who was condemned
to death partly because he had not cried at his mother's
funeral.

The Islands of Unwisdom (1949)

The Islands of Unwisdom is a somewhat depressing
account of a sixteenth century expedition to colonize the

Solomon Islands. The leader of the expedition, Don Alvaro de Mendaña y Castro, had discovered the islands many years before. He called them the Isles of Solomon, thinking perhaps they were the location of the famous gold mines of the biblical King Solomon. Certainly, the natives adorned themselves with gold. When the Spanish king finally gives his permission for the expedition, therefore, a great many avaricious participants join in a venture ostensibly devoted to Christianizing the heathen.

Though a few devout persons, such as the three priests and the chief pilot, Don Pedro Fernández, try to maintain the Christian charity of their mission, their feeble efforts are in vain. Practically all the islanders greet them with affection and open hospitality, but sooner or later some senseless slaughter of innocents converts friends into enemies. The combined stupidity and violence of the military and of the three Barretos, Don Alvaro's brothers-in-law, insure disaster wherever they go. Moreover, Doña Ysabel Barreto, Don Alvaro's beautiful wife, is as proud and cruel as her arrogant brothers. Don Alvaro is devout but indecisive and unable to control the stubborn wills that surround him. Meanwhile, the commander of the military forces, Colonel Don Pedro de Manrique, though a brave man, usually acts on impulse and, if drunk, can be quite oblivious to the most disastrous consequences.

The narrator, Don Andrés Serrano, an undersecretary to the general, explains that one reason for the nautical superiority of the English over the Spanish is the rigid class structure of the latter. The English soldier can and will do a sailor's work, but the Spanish soldier does nothing but fight. During a long and hazardous voyage, the Spanish soldier is idle and bored, while the sailor is overworked and resentful. When at last a new land is reached, the soldier seems bound to justify his existence by killing enemies. If none exist, he soon creates them.

The expedition never reaches the Isles of Solomon, but tries to plant a colony on another island the general names Santa Cruz. This venture might have survived, at least, had not Doña Ysabel bribed a soldier to kill the chieftain. This crime she uses as an excuse to charge the colonel with plotting a revolt against her husband. (The colonel had earned the hatred of the proud Barreto family on several occasions.) Don Alvaro stands weakly by while the Barreto brothers execute the colonel and his cronies without trial.

Not only do the natives now attack the would-be colonists at every opportunity, but tropical fevers also begin killing off the Spaniards at an alarming rate. The general sickens and dies, willing his command to his wife.

Eventually, the ragged remnant set sail in their rotting vessels, but without adequate supplies. After many hardships, especially thirst and starvation, the chief pilot brings the flagship, the only remaining of four vessels, into Manila Bay. Of the settlers, all of the children and most of the men and women, have died. The only really healthy persons are Doña Ysabel and one surviving brother, who have hoarded supplies while the others died miserably.

A historical epilogue explains that it was almost two hundred years before the Isles of Solomon were rediscovered. So dreary is this account that the reader can only applaud, on behalf of the natives, this blessed reprieve from the greed and folly of Christians.

This ferociously unromantic view of sixteenth century adventurers is probably fairly accurate as to the grimmer details of shipboard existence and colonization. Nor is the brutality toward the Indians anything new, since the Spanish had already displayed their special brand of piety in Mexico and South America. The one unprecedented feature of this particular case was that a woman achieved the command of a naval vessel.

This is probably the fact that most intrigued Graves and the one that he embroidered with some imagination. This novel came out, incidentally, the year following *The White Goddess*. Though the real Doña Ysabel must, indeed, have been unusually independent, Graves makes her the veritable incarnation of the White Goddess in her most sinister aspect.

Transposing the novel into mythic terms, the Goddess's Sacred King is impotent. Don Alvaro, who is much older than his wife, makes a vow of celibacy until such time that he sets foot on the Isles of Solomon. He even assumes the garb of a monk. The discomfiture this must occasion for the fiery Doña Ysabel is the subject of secret jokes among the sailors.

The White Goddess always sacrifices the Old King, symbolic of the waning year. Many of the more ignorant sailors and soldiers think Doña Ysabel is a witch and a moon-worshipper. Presumably, she at least played on her husband's superstitious fears to bring about his death. The native chieftain had changed names with the general to show their brotherhood. Thus, when the chieftain dies, by Doña Ysabel's contriving, the general, already weakened by fever, believes he is doomed by sympathetic magic.

When the Goddess is thus freed from the old, she demands the love and allegiance of a new Sacred King, symbolic of the waxing year. Doña Ysabel seduces the chief pilot, after several bald-faced lies—including that her late husband had a letter before he left Peru, saying that the Pilot's wife had died. The General destroyed the letter, she says, because he was afraid of losing his navigator. Needless to say, poor Pedro Fernandez is completely taken in by her deceit.

After the new Sacred King has served his function as consort, the love Goddess again reveals her Persephone or Hecate aspect. After a brief passionate interlude when Doña Ysabel steals nightly into Don Pedro's room, she suddenly comes no more and treats him with extreme coldness. She has accomplished her purpose, which is to conceive a child, who will be acknowledged as her husband's. Only thus can she hope to keep her husband's ancestral titles and possessions in her own family. Pedro Fernández is left puzzled and chagrined by her rejection. He knows he can say nothing without risking death as a seducer at the hands of her hot-headed brothers.

Since Doña Ysabel miscarries this child, and the chief

pilot is neither her social equal nor actually a widower, the White Goddess finds a new rich consort in Manila. As a matter of fact, our narrator assures us that her character changed completely, and that thereafter she became a good wife to her second husband. What this may suggest is that her role as the fatal woman was largely Graves's addition to an interesting historical fact. I dare say, the log book kept by Andrés Serrano never divulged what Doña Ysabel said to the Chief Pilot in the privacy of his bed.

Perhaps Graves was simply in a bitter mood when writing this novel, as he must have been when composing the poem "Return." After contemplating an appropriate revenge upon the woman who has kept him in misery for years, the persona in the poem relents:

> But no, I ask a surer peace
> Than vengeance on you could provide.
> So fear no ill from my release:
> Be off, elude the curse, disgrace
> Some other green and happy place—
> This world of fools is wide.

For all of that, Graves probably made the right choice to enliven the wretchedness of this journey with some love interest. If it were not all so heavy and masochistic in effect, it might evoke in the reader's memory the more comic bedroom scene in *Sir Gawain and the Green Knight*. Like Sir Gawain, the righteous Don Pedro Fernandez is constrained by the rules of courtly love (which always subtly compromised Christian sexual morality) to serve the lord's lady in whatever way she demands. When the lady comes to his bedside and asks to be comforted, what is a gentleman to do? But Graves poured all the comic possibilities of female dominance into *Watch the North Wind Rise*, which came out the same year. That fantasy also has a bedroom scene where a witch masquerades as a wife.

The Islands of Unwisdom is neither comedy nor tragedy, but rather almost unrelieved pessimism. Tragedy, after all, implies some grandeur that has gone wrong. There is little grandeur in the pious ineptitude of Don Alvaro, little nobility in the pampered Doña Ysabel, little gallantry in the pompous colonel or in the arrogant brothers. And the chief pilot, for all his good impulses, hardly measures up to a tragic hero. One might piously accept the dying vicar's judgment that God was punishing them all for their sins. One might less piously wish that God could become as adept at prevention as He is at punishment.

The Story of Marie Powell, Wife to Mr. Milton (1943)

Wife to Mr. Milton is the story of a bad marriage— Marie Powell and John Milton did not "fadge." The glossary at the end of the novel, to aid the reader with seventeenth-century diction, reveals that "fadge" means "agree." Context suggests, however, that it refers to general compatibility more than to simple agreement in an argument. And it was this same Marie Powell who inspired John Milton to write his somewhat notorious pamphlet claiming incompatibility should be sufficient grounds for divorce— this at a time when adultery was the usual justification.

The sixteen-year-old Marie agrees to marry Mr. Milton, then thirty-two, for the sake of her family. Powell wishes to borrow money from Milton. Moreover, the impending civil war between King Charles and his rebellious parliament suggests that an alliance with the prominent poet and writer might be a hedge against disaster.

Another reason for her compliance is that her one true love, Edmund Verney, called Mun, is reported to be engaged to marry his own cousin. Marie had fallen in love with Mun at the tender age of eleven. Actually, they had seen each other only rarely, but they had both become aware of a degree of secret empathy that can only be called mental telepathy. Mun suggests perhaps they knew each other in former lives, explaining the theory of transmigration of souls advanced by Pythagoras. Mun is now far away, however, as a loyalist soldier, and Marie believes their love is never destined to be other than platonic.

The marriage to Milton is a disaster from the very beginning. A misunderstanding, which Marie cannot correct because of Milton's imperious order to keep silent, causes her exile from his bed as punishment for her supposed rebelliousness. Marie is still a virgin when, to bring her to repentance, Milton sends her back to her father with orders to return at Michaelmas-tide, with the money Mr. Powell still owes him.

Marie is overjoyed to escape from this gloomy household and its petty tyrant to the freedom of her father's country estate. Meanwhile, civil war breaks out in earnest. Marie's parents agree to use the real danger to a young woman traveling in a countryside swarming with soldiers as an excuse to keep her home, in spite of Milton's summons to return. Thus, the visit extends to three years. It is during this interval that the frustrated Milton publishes his treatise on divorce.

Yet Marie returns to London at last, for General Cromwell's forces are obviously winning over the king's men. She correctly perceives that her loyalist father will be ruined when the king surrenders. Her alliance with the prominent Puritan may save her family.

Milton begrudgingly accepts her back, in spite of the fact that the money her father owes is never paid. Moreover, he does help the family when Powell is thrown out of his estate. It is a joyless marriage, however, especially when their first two children are girls. Milton obviously considers women to be only chattels.

When Marie is four months pregnant with her third child, she collapses suddenly in the street and is unconscious for three days. By her own account, she spent those three days with Mun, "a lifetime of happiness." When she regains consciousness, she knows that Mun was killed in Ireland at the moment when she fainted away. The child she subsequently bears, a son at last, looks like Mun, and Marie is more content than she has ever been. The epilogue discloses that Marie died after giving birth to a fourth child, a girl, and the one son died about six weeks later.

Though some readers may find the style of this novel somewhat ponderous, Graves tries to adjust his diction, to some extent, to the times. Certainly, the somewhat oppressive formality of Milton's speech seems justified, considering Milton's own writing style. Graves has deliberately employed some archaic terms, though their meaning is clear in context. The glossary at the end is not really necessary. It may be mostly for "show," offered as rebuttal to objections before they are made, or perhaps simply as a demonstration of his research into seventeenth-century diction.

The characterization of Milton is, in some ways, more distinct and consistent than that of Marie Powell, the narrator. He is a domestic tyrant who officiously supports his dominant rule with scriptural references. This Puritan severity is not shown as the whole of Milton's personality, to be sure. By implication, Milton is at war with his own softer impulses. More than once, Marie senses that Milton is drawn to her more than he is willing to admit. But this impulse he perceives as a weakness or sin, like Adam's uxoriousness, which brings about the fall of man in *Paradise Lost.* He overcompensates so successfully for this tendency that the result is consistently grim.

This is one novel in which Graves obviously displays his personal bias. Though the political issues of this turbulent period are underplayed, Milton is deliberately, some may say viciously, maligned. Graves reveals this most surely in his comments on Milton's writing. Graves seems to go out of his way to suggest that Milton's "Comus" is derivative; that politics, not friendship, inspired "Lycidas"; that the divorce paper is misleading. Moreover, he notes that Milton himself became a government censor for the Commonwealth, in spite of the admirable sentiments in his essay called "Areopagitica," decrying censorship of the press. The fact that Milton criticizes the poet John Skelton suggests a fundamental difference in attitude and judgment from Graves. John Skelton has been Graves's special favorite among English poets. Whether or not these objections to Milton are legitimate, they certainly show an unusual emotional involvement on Graves's part in the subject of his novel. It is all the more noticeable because he usually maintains considerable distance from the characters and issues that he describes.[1]

Perhaps it is to Graves's credit that Marie Powell seems to be a fairly passive housewife, in spite of her supposed independence of mind. Graves has refrained from misrepresenting her as some kind of successful adversary to Milton, which, in some ways, would make better "theater." Milton does not really have a shrew to tame.

Graves does take care to suggest a basic contrast in lifestyle between Milton's joyless existence and the peculiar mixture of pagan and Christian folkways that Marie comes from. And there is more than a little implication that the trouble lies in the old issue of male dominance, or its unhealthy exaggeration in Milton's brand of Christianity.

Ironically, it is not Milton but Marie's mother, a forceful, dominating woman, who explains to her daughter the "proper" role of woman in marriage:

"Remember," said she, "that Eve was formed of Adam's rib, not from the bones of his head, and that therefore woman cannot presume to argue with man. Man was created the perfect creature, and not the woman with him at the same time, as happened with both sexes of other creatures; nor was she made to be his equal, but for his use and benefit, as his servant. You must look to your husband evermore to reverence him and obey him, and please him, and sail by no other compass than that of his direction. If he be angered with you, rest not until you have pacified him; and if he blame you without a cause, bear it patiently without an unkind word, and rather take the fault upon yourself than seem to be displeased. Oh, may the Lord give you a patient command of yourself to do nothing that will discontent him! Avoid idleness, avoid vain babbling and a proud carriage, preserve a decent sadness in your behavior and apparel, give yourself to honest exercises—to spinning, sewing, washing, wringing, sweeping, scouring and the like. If your husband praise you, let your heart sing. Put off the tom-boy, put on the grave matron. Go not from the house except as he give you leave; for the cock flies abroad to bring in, and the hen sits upon the nest to keep all at home. Marriage is a grievous condition for a woman, but honorable; for though she be by nature weaker than a man, both in mind and in body, yet she is an excellent instrument for him if she yield herself wholly."

Upon delivering this dismal sermon, Mrs. Powell leaves the room to take over from her ineffectual husband the haggling with Milton over dowry and other legal matters. Both Mrs. Powell and her daughter share the view that a woman accommodates herself to such dreary doctrine only so much as absolutely necessary for survival. Given half a chance, a woman can find ways to maintain her dignity, but Milton seems to close every avenue of self-respect for Marie.

Milton, then, is condemned partly because he chooses Jehovah, metaphorically speaking, and tries to demote Eve. From Graves's point of view, the Christian poet must be passionately devoted to Eve (or perhaps the Virgin Mary), since she is the Christian transformation of the ancient White Goddess. As Graves has noted elsewhere, even Milton's honorific term for Eve in *Paradise Lost*, Mother of All Mankind, originally designated the Goddess. Milton, as a poet of great power, is thus a traitor to the Muse and deserves the misery of an incompatible wife.

In another reading of the same situation, Milton has chosen the head over the heart. Though he desires love, like any man, he has a preconceived set of rules that would define and coerce love, which can only be freely given. He resolutely divorces sexuality from pleasurable impulse, for instance, knowing his wife only when trying to impregnate her—in compliance, presumably, to God's orders. Such dominance of head over heart is self-destructive.

The most entertaining parts of the novel are perhaps the early descriptions of rural England with its somewhat pagan love of dancing and masquerades, the tradition of hospitality and festival. The Lord of Misrule still holds sway during festival times. In a delightful scene during a masquerade, Mr. Powell's services are required in his role of judge. He therefore comes away from the party in his devil costume, attended by his young sons, dressed as monkeys, to hold court. The unfortunate miscreant will probably never forget the terror of that trial before the devil.

The touch of the supernatural provided in the mystical communion between Marie and Mun suggests a happier destiny than the bare facts of history can entertain. Nature still holds to her secret purposes, no matter what rationalizations men construct to change them. Here, Graves the poet speaks, not Graves the researcher into curious episodes of the historical past.

13

Historical Novels:
on Two Soldiers: Sergeant
Lamb,
and Count Belisarius

Roger Lamb's America (1940) and
Proceed, Sergeant Lamb (1941)

Roger Lamb's America (in England, *Sergeant Lamb of the Ninth*) traces the career of a young Irishman who fought in the British army in America during the American revolution. He shares the misery of boot camp with another young man named Richard Harlowe, who becomes his rival for the hand of the beautiful Kate Weldone. Kate marries Harlowe, however, and goes to America with him when the troops are ordered to Canada to help quell the revolt of the American colonists. They land in Quebec in 1776. Lamb avoids Harlowe and his bride, since he is having difficulty recovering from unrequited love.

He becomes a good friend of the Mohican war chief Thayendanegea, called Captain Brant by the English, who is an ally of the English against the American colonists. Since the British are ignorant of the forest and the unorthodox methods of fighting used by colonists and Indians, Roger Lamb and his friend Terry Reeves are ordered to travel with the Indians and learn their forest wisdom and fighting methods, in order to advise the British troops. Lamb thoroughly enjoys this experience, and Thayendanegea adopts him into the Mohican tribe.

Kate Harlowe has not yet dropped out of Lamb's life. While performing a military errand, Sergeant Lamb discovers a group of Indians arguing about which of two suitors should marry a weeping white woman, who is none other than the beautiful Kate. She had run away from her churlish husband, thoroughly regretting that she had not chosen Roger instead, and had intended to throw herself over Niagara Falls. An Indian transvestite, Sweet Yellow Head, had approached her and offered her sympathy and the protection of a group of Ottawa traveling into the state of New York. Actually, she had been very well treated by them; her present predicament arose from her ignorance of the proper way to discourage two young chiefs who had fallen in love with her. Now that Thayendanegea is in control of the situation, he obligingly marries the rescued Kate to Sergeant Lamb in a native ceremony.

Kate is pregnant when this idyllic interlude comes to a close. The time comes for Lamb to return to his regiment, where Kate is well known as married to Harlowe, from whom she has never been divorced. Though Generals Howe and Burgoyne were known to consort with other men's wives, such conduct was not condoned among enlisted men. Kate gives her lover a choice: either he can desert his role as soldier and live with her in the wilderness with their Indian friends, or he must say goodbye to her forever and never lay claim to the child she carries. He sadly chooses his duty as a British soldier, and Kate goes quietly back to the Indians.

Actually this love affair provides only a tenuous thread on which to hang some plot. Most of the book is devoted to details of military life, curious anecdotes about the colonists, the Indians, the French Canadians, the fiascos and triumphs of generals. (Benedict Arnold seems to be the most admired of the American generals, though Washington earns some respect from the English.) At the end of the novel Sergeant Lamb and his fellow soldiers of the Ninth Regiment have been captured by the colonists.

This story is not "straight history," Graves explains in his foreword, though he has invented no main characters.

The reader has no way of knowing exactly how accurately he conveys the texture of life in the colonies. "All that readers of an historical novel can fairly ask from the author," he writes, "is an assurance that he has nowhere wilfully falsified geography, chronology, or character, and that the information contained in it is accurate enough to add without discount to their general stock of history."

Perhaps the main difficulty of the novel is the failure to establish reader involvement, because of the cool detachment of the autobiographical voice and the relative unimportance of plot. It seems to be a scholar's compilation of interesting anecdotes and factual data about the time. Of course, this unimpassioned tone could be defended as exactly appropriate, since presumably it is written as a memoir by a much older Roger Lamb when he is a schoolmaster in Dublin. Thus, Graves prudently covers the shortcomings of the story as a novel with the somewhat didactic purpose of an aging schoolmaster. Yet, this cool distance is the same kind of reserve one perceives even in Graves's own wartime autobiography, *Goodbye to All That*. No one gets really close to Graves or shares his mental life, even when he writes most precisely of his own experience. Nor does one feel really close to Sergeant Lamb, nor care much whether he chooses love or duty.

Proceed, Sergeant Lamb provides the further adventures of this intrepid young Irishman. Most of the book involves detailed accounts of daring escapes from imprisonment and harrowing flights across enemy countryside to English-held territory. One admires the young man's endurance, ingenuity, and bravery, extricating himself and a few companions from one dangerous predicament after another. There are also occasional glimpses of well-known persons, such as the handsome Major André whom Washington felt compelled to hang as a spy, because he was caught out of uniform and involved in the defection of Benedict Arnold.

Sergeant Lamb has a brief unexpected meeting with

his old flame, Kate Harlowe, who had been told that he was
dead. She is now mistress of Lord Cornwallis. His renewed
hope of an alliance with Kate is dashed forever when she is
killed in the subsequent bombardment of Yorktown by
General Washington and the Marquis de La Fayette. Lamb
eventually marries another young women, Jane Crummer,
widowed by the war, who had conducted herself with great
bravery and fortitude under fire and imprisonment. Much
later, when he is a schoolmaster in Ireland, Lamb is visited
by his long lost daughter, Kate's child, who has been reared
by a kindly American Quaker.

Although these novels do not achieve the vitality and
color of *I, Claudius* and *Count Belisarius*, they are an
interesting addition to the small group of novels available in
America that treat our revolution from the loyalist point of
view. They thus help mitigate some of the romantic biases
Americans may have of that period. Graves, however, is no
polemicist. In fact, he seems to have only an academic
interest in the political controversies of that contest.

The real clue to his interest in the subject is the illus-
trious history of the Royal Welsh Fusiliers. Sergeant Lamb,
though originally of the Ninth, joined the Fusiliers after
one of his daring escapes. The Ninth had been incarcerated
when General Burgoyne surrendered. Graves was, of
course, a member of the Royal Welsh Fusiliers in World
War I and has a proprietary interest in their history. Moreover, as he explains in the preface to *Proceed, Sergeant
Lamb*, his great-grandfather and grandfather were Dublin-
ers of Lamb's day. Two other relatives were admirals who
commanded British fleets in American waters.

The preface to *Proceed, Sergeant Lamb* is more expan-
sive about the sources of the historical information contained in the two books. One is grateful for this courtesy, for
sometimes Graves seems to suggest that the whole question
of historical accuracy is an issue that no reader has the right
to ask. He has more than once implied that his stories could
be profusely documented, but that he has no intention of
doing so.

Count Belisarius (1938)

The main attraction of *Count Belisarius* is that it illuminates a period of history that most readers know nothing about. In the sixth century A.D. Constantinople, not Rome, was the most powerful center of civilization, barbarian hordes still threatened the Christian world, and the precise nature of Christ's divinity was still a matter of heated controversy. Belisarius was a remarkably bold and resourceful cavalry commander in the service of the Byzantine Emperor Justinian. His military genius not only repelled invasions from Persia, but also reconquered that part of the western empire that had fallen to the Vandals and Goths swarming down from Europe. Moreover, he was, at least according to Graves's novel, a supremely honorable man in a corrupt world.

The narrator of the story is a eunuch named Eugenius, who is a trusted servant of Belisarius's wife Antonina. He has only a minor role in the action but his narrative function is important. One so modest as Belisarius might model his account on Caesar's succinct "I came, I saw, I conquered." But a man who is a hero to his own slave comes highly recommended indeed. Nonetheless, the account is not heightened into melodrama, as well it might be in other hands, but is a sober and factual account of the life of a man of action.

The combination of masculinity, Christian sentiment, and Roman virtue that is Belisarius is set off by two somewhat pagan, exotic women, good-hearted when not crossed, but bred to be entertainers and prostitutes. These two friends, Antonina and Theodora, give up prostitution and adopt Christianity as a matter of expedience, when it becomes possible to marry prominant Christians. Antonina first marries a merchant sufficiently rich to improve her social position and sufficiently old to suggest early widowhood. A disastrous earthquake relieves her of this husband. After that she marries Belisarius, who had met her once when they were both very young and she an acrobatic

dancer at a banquet he attended. Belisarius had declared his
love for her even then and had presumably been remarkably
chaste ever since. This essential difference between his strict
religious views of sexual ethics and Antonina's more relaxed
pagan acceptance of sexuality seems to cause very little
trouble in the family. As a matter of fact, Antonina is a very
good and faithful wife to Belisarius, accompanying him on
his campaigns and even playing an active part in defensive
fighting when Belisarius is short-handed—which is most of
the time.

Theodora also marries a devout, but otherwise vain
and unpleasant, Christian who comes under her spell. In
one sense, she could hardly have done better, for her husband becomes the Emperor Justinian. Fortunately, both for
her sake and for Antonina and Belisarius, Justinian never
completely escapes her influence. More than once Theodora saves Belisarius from the vindictive jealousy of Justinian, or convinces the negligent monarch that he should
send some relief in troops or supplies to his champion on
the frontier. When Belisarius makes urgent pleas for military support, since he is invariably greatly outnumbered by
his enemies, Justinian is likely to treat them very cavalierly.
But Antonina sends, at the same time, a private letter to the
Empress Theodora, explaining the military situation.
Theodora, by flattery or guile, usually can cajole Justinian
into at least some action not utterly disastrous.

Mostly, however, Belisarius learns to depend upon his
wits and his personal band of highly trained cavalry armed
with superior bows. He has taught them to shoot accurately
from swiftly moving horses, an art which is quite beyond the
skill of the enemy tribes. When faced with the dubious help
of raw recruits, perhaps desperate peasants gathered from the
countryside, he teaches them to do one thing supremely
well. He then deploys them in exactly the situation in
which that one skill is effective. One way or another, his
meager hundreds or thousands prevail over tens of thousands, and he gets a reputation as a worker of miracles. The

expedition against Carthage, the defeat of the Vandals, the siege of Naples, the taking of Rome from the Goths, and its defense when the Goths return in greater numbers than ever before—whatever is necessary Belisarius can do.

Ultimately it is his success that destroys him, and his emperor who is his worst enemy. The court at Constantinople is, of course, infested with ambitious men. Several of them plot to discredit Belisarius and seem to show that he has designs on the throne. Schemers have already slandered Antonina to her husband, offering seemingly adequate proofs of her infidelity. Belisarius is so shocked that he discards her in a rage. Meanwhile, Theodora has died. Now there is no buffer to the envy and hatred of Justinian, who has always feared him, because he is loved by the people and idolized by his soldiers. Belisarius is briefly imprisoned, his wealth confiscated, and he is blinded—a bitter reward for a lifetime of service.

Antonina, at first vindictive when Belisarius rejects her, now in abject grief sends Eugenius to serve him when he is released from prison. Belisarius goes to sit before the monastery of Job the Prophet to beg alms. He cries out "spare a copper for Belisarius who once scattered gold in these streets!" The populace recognize him with awe, and they file past his begging bowl all day, each giving what he can. Moreover, rude scrawls appear on the public buildings about blind Samson who destroyed a king and his court.

Justinian is more terrified than ever and hastens to pardon Belisarius and restore his titles and property. All devious plots are finally exposed. Antonina is reconciled to her husband and nurses him tenderly for the few weeks of life that remain to him. His final days are serene. His old soldiers visit his house continually to talk over old campaigns. Even now, his example humiliates Justinian, for Belisarius seems effortlessly to hold court for all the loyal and the brave.

Though there is little plot, in the usual sense, to this novel, the action is so exciting and colorful that it seems to make little difference. Graves is adept at delineating the styles and unique skills of the different tribes and the strategic methods of Belisarius in meeting each situation. Most of the book is continual warfare, but it is also a continual travelog of strange people and places out of our largely forgotten past.

A profound irony permeates the novel, for all Belisarius's miracle-working comes to very little in the end. Not because of Justinian's wretched treatment of Belisarius, but because the remarkable gains in empire that Belisarius achieves are soon lost. Justinian, fearing to create another champion so powerful as Belisarius, foolishly divides the command among a flock of petty generals. They are so fragmented that they are often easy prey for the vigorous Goths. And Constantinople itself is almost lost when the Persians swarm into the country after Justinian has removed Belisarius from command. The hero's last military venture, before his imprisonment and blinding, is to rally his old soldiers in the defense of the city—without the aid and blessing of Justinian, who is paralyzed with indecision and spends his time praying. Although the Persians are once again beaten and turned away, this presumption of authority seals Belisarius's fate and leads to his trial for treason.

In the midst of all this valor, there is perhaps a less obvious irony, nowhere overtly suggested. It is, of course, the futility of war, its incredible waste, its unscrupulous sacrifice of the lives of thousands for the ambitions of a few, its glorification of destruction in the name of true religion. Though the Christian hero offers an example of humaneness to the defeated foe, the men he kills are just as dead. One suspects that the Graves who lived the horror of trench warfare in World War I has something to do with this half-admiring, half-ironic view of the military hero. Yet the irony is never a matter of discernible tone, but rather the reader's final judgment. Thus, under the general theme of the novel, the plight of the good man in an evil world, lurks a more subtle underlying question—what does it mean to be good?

It is perhaps unfair, when a writer does many things very well, to wish that he were more perfect in yet another way. One wishes that Graves were as skillful with psychological and philosophical implications of his subject matter as he is with the telling of events. Certainly the career of Belisarius, like that of Claudius, could be the stuff of a literary masterpiece. If the human insights of Shakespeare and Tolstoy, say, could just be added to the scholarship and story-telling talent of Graves, how overwhelming might be the result!

But we must be thankful for the considerable gifts that Graves displays. He lets us live in an alien world, very different from ours in some details, yet depressingly alike in others. We see that power, as usual, corrupts. Yet, there are special people who seem to be immune to that rule. We could ponder the reason for that immunity, which is not really made clear. Is it his heritage of Roman stoicism or his Christianity or some happy accident of the genes that makes Belisarius impervious to vice, fraud, and pride? We do not know.

It is a world in which Christian religious doctrine has not yet crystallized into convention. Where merchants and diplomats may argue vehemently over the single or double nature of Christ. Such earnest discussions go on even in the entertainment houses. One of the charms of Theodora to Justinian is her perceptive understanding of Christian doctrine. He casts her in the role of Mary Magdalene, who was also a reformed prostitute. According to rumor, however, even as empress, she sacrifices occasionally to Hecate, the witch goddess of the dark of the moon.

It is a world, in other words, where one makes religious decisions from an array of radically different possibilities. Our pallid preferences for Protestant or Catholic or Jew, or perhaps watered-down Zen, American Muslim, or Korean Moonie seem blurred and inconsequential indeed compared with the intellectual risks of the early medieval milieu.

The rather obvious moral casting of Belisarius and Justinian as good and evil is heightened by the superstitious rumors about Justinian. Some claim he sold his soul to the devil, and a fortune teller warns Theodora early-on that she will marry the devil. But Justinian's shortcomings actually seem far more plausible than Belisarius's virtue.

Some critics have complained of a certain woodenness in the character of Belisarius. They are, unfortunately, quite right. One sees his public actions, but little or nothing of his emotions or motivations, his doubts or fears, if, indeed, he ever had any. He seems larger than life in his accomplishments, yet smaller than life for the conspicuous absence of contradictions in his character—no secret doubts, no moral ambiguities, no mental suffering.

But in spite of these limitations of character development, this is one of the best of Graves's historical novels.

14

Historical Novels:
on Claudius

I, Claudius and *Claudius the God* (both 1934)

For that elite group who have read the Roman historians, particularly the *Annals of Tacitus* and Suetonius's *Lives of the Twelve Caesars*, Graves's two novels about imperial Rome may seem like twice-told tales. But for the rest of us, which means almost everybody, *I, Claudius* and *Claudius the God* provide a unique insight into first-century Rome and a somber commentary upon human corruptibility.

Claudius, born in 10 B.C., was a grandchild of Mark Antony and a grand nephew of Octavius Augustus, who ruled as emperor throughout Claudius's childhood and early manhood. Augustus had become a virtual ruler in Italy by 37 B.C., but was officially the emperor from 23 B.C. to his death in 14 A.D.

Perhaps the most surprising fact about Claudius is that he managed to stay alive through not only Augustus's long reign but also through that of his successors, Tiberius and Caligula. Most members of the royal family died prematurely of unnatural causes, as real or fancied threats to someone's political ambitions.

The first novel, *I, Claudius*, concerns the narrator's life up to the point when he is swept dramatically into power after the assassination of Caligula. *Claudius the God* carries him through his career as emperor until, like so many before him, he is poisoned by an unscrupulous and ambitious woman.

Claudius's physical deformity, the curse that blights his childhood, is paradoxically his blessing also. Because of it, no one considers him a competitor for power. He calls himself "the cripple, the stammerer, the fool of the family." His legs are defective, one shorter than the other, so he moves very awkwardly. Hs has a painful stammer that makes conversation uncomfortable. He drools at the mouth when he sleeps. Even his mother considers him stupid, and his grandmother Livia refuses to have him in the same room with her. The Emperor Augustus, whom he idolizes, is uncomfortable when Claudius is around. He has few close friends, for the handsome young noblemen he grows up with despise him. It is small wonder that he becomes a somewhat solitary bookish person. The probable misery of such a childhood, however, is never very prominent in the account. He learns stoicism early.

Claudius is not totally lacking affectionate companions, however. His dependence on their love is the more pathetic when one after another they are sent away or murdered. He finds a friend in one old scholar, Athenadoras, who recognizes that he is not so stupid as he seems and has a positive talent for history. Augustus's grandson Postumus also treats him kindly. But his greatest champion, who defends him against the bullying of other children, is his brother Germanicus, whom he loves dearly.

When Claudius is thirteen years old, he tastes the first of many bitter tragedies. He falls in love with a lovely young girl, Medullina Camilla, who perceives the sensitive, intelligent boy beneath the physical deformities. Claudius arranges that the girl be promised to him for wife. On the very day of the betrothal, however, the girl dies of poison. Grandmother Livia apparently fears that the offspring of this particular match might create a competitor for her son Tiberius as successor to Augustus.

Claudius is then betrothed against his will to a monstrous young woman of almost superhuman strength, six feet three inches and still growing. His first thought on seeing her is "This woman is capable of murder by violence"—a statement prophetic of the future. Urgulanilla is the first of four wives Claudius has during his life, all of them treacherous, unfaithful, and sometimes murderous.

Grandmother Livia, Augustus's wife, who arranges the death of Claudius's first love, pulls the strings in an incredible web of intrigue that entangles one after another of Claudius's friends and acquaintances. She is determined that Tiberius, her son by a former marriage, shall inherit the throne. Augustus, however, has a daughter, Julia, by a former marriage, who in turn has five children, all of whom are closer to the throne than Tiberius. Julia becomes embroiled in scandals, real or created by Livia, and is finally banished by her father. Two of the sons, Gaius and Lucius, die of unknown causes. One of Julia's daughters, Agrippina, marries Claudius's brother Germanicus and accompanies him to the frontier in Germany. The other daughter is banished on a trumped-up charge of adultery because she is going to bear a child who would be a great-grandson of Augustus.

Finally, even Postumus, Julia's last son and one of Claudius's few friends, suffers banishment, through the conniving of Livia and Livilla, Claudius's sister. When Germanicus returns from the wars, Claudius convinces him that Postumus was framed, and Germanicus in turn convinces Augustus of that fact.

For the first time Augustus does something behind Livia's back. He goes in secret and rescues his grandson from his island prison, putting in his place a slave named Clement, who resembles Postumus. At the same time, he changes all the guards on the island. Clement is promised his freedom for playing this part. (It is a poor bargain, for he is murdered after Augustus dies.)

Livia finds out about this deception through her spy network, but feigns ignorance. It is the beginning of the end for Augustus, however. He begins to fail in health, presumably because of slow poisons administered by his wife, and dies at last in Livia's loving arms. Honest Germanicus is conveniently absent, fighting again in Germany. Tiberius, who is no longer young, makes a great show of reluctance at assuming leadership of the state, but, of course, he is finally convinced of his duty. After all, who else is available? Tiberius eventually captures Postumus, who has been in hiding, and has him tortured and executed without public trial.

In constant fear now of poisoning, Claudius falls ill. His painful stammer returns, and a certain aphasia makes him worthless in the position of priest, which is the only public office he was thought competent to perform.

He never sees Germanicus again, for Germanicus dies under strange circumstances after much mental anguish. Germanicus had been sent away again, to the east this time, with his wife and his eight-year-old son Caligula. His mysterious death occurs after a weird campaign of terror that preys upon his superstitious nature. He finds all kinds of grisly objects hidden under loose tiles in the floor and in the walls—the corpse of a cat, the body of a dead baby, a negro's severed head with a child's hand protruding from its mouth—always with the name Germanicus scrawled nearby. The reader does not find out until close to the end of the novel that the perpetrator of these horrors is Germanicus's own son, Caligula, an early indication of the insanity and depravity of his short reign as Tiberius's successor.

When Tiberius dies at last, the people are glad to hail the twenty-five year old Caligula as the new emperor, partly because they had disliked Tiberius, partly because they had idolized Caligula's father Germanicus as a folk hero. Moreover, Caligula gives away gold with a free hand to his enthusiastic supporters.

This early generosity, however, soon proves to be a talent for squandering fabulous sums of money. Indeed, in the few wild years of his reign Caligula practically bankrupts the government with spectacular and often cruel displays to feed his megalomania. His most spectacular extravagance is a wild project of making a bridge of ships across the Bay of Baiae, because some former senator had once remarked that he (Caligula) "could no more become emperor than ride a horse across the Bay of Baiae." He commandeers about 4000 vessels, including a thousand built for the purpose, and has them anchored in a double line from the decks of Puteoli to his villa at Bauli. He chops off the high sterns, connects the ships with boards, and covers them with earth until he has a solid highway across the bay. When trading vessels appear, he appropriates them and makes them into islands with gardens. All this, in order that he might have a magnificent parade, he himself wearing the breastplate of Alexander the Great, Julius Caesar's sword, the reputed battle-ax of Romulus, and the reputed shield of Aeneas.

Ironically, Caligula rescues his uncle Claudius from the political obscurity that has always been his lot. For the first time Claudius is favored with public offices, but mostly to serve as the butt of Caligula's cruel humor. Instead of enhancing Claudius's security, Caligula's attention only brings him closer to the unstable and explosive center of power. More than once, Claudius escapes death only by his wits, turning away Caligula's malice with flattery or making a joke of his own misery, awkwardness, or ineptitude.

At last, Caligula is brutally murdered by a group of his subordinates. His wife and child are immediately butchered as well. Poor uncle Claudius, hiding behind some draperies in the palace, figures his time has come. The crowd, however, in a rowdy good mood as they are looting the palace, discover the trembling Claudius, hoist him up on their shoulders and shout "Long live Emperor Claudius!"

Thus ends the subjugation of Claudius, the fool of the family, and a new career of power begins. *I, Claudius* ends at that climactic point in the palace when the terrified Claudius is being borne on the shoulders of the palace guards.

Claudius the God recounts both the positive accomplishments of Claudius's reign and some of his more subtle failures. Claudius, inheriting a bankrupt and disordered state, works hard at a number of worthwhile projects. He replenishes the treasury by melting down gold statues and monuments that Caligula had erected for his own greater glory. He builds aqueducts (some of which still stand). He creates a harbor and lighthouse at Ostia, which can be used in the winter to bring in much-needed grain from Africa.

He also successfully invades Britain, an endeavor not so obviously vital to the people he serves. As a matter of fact, Claudius wants a triumph, the magnificent parade and pageant for a military hero. Both Augustus and Tiberius had been great generals in their younger days, but Claudius had never proved himself by the standards of a society that glorified war.

Claudius's reign is not without dangers of a more subtle nature than those of the battlefield, however. Though perceptive in so many ways, Claudius is sometimes blind about what is going on in the palace. He comes near to meeting his earlier reputation for foolishness, because of his naïvety about his beautiful wife Messalina. He is perhaps personally saddened, but not at all suspicious, when dear Messalina asks for separate quarters in the palace, at some distance from his own. She is not long in developing her own pernicious system of political graft, arranging some assassinations, and obtaining bed partners more attractive than the aging Claudius. All of Rome knows of her corruption and licentiousness except the emperor.

Claudius at last discovers a plot to overthrow his government, led by his wife and one of her lovers. He takes prompt action to eliminate the plotters, including Messalina, but he is emotionally shattered by her betrayal.

After this devastating episode, Claudius goes through a painful period of reassessing his experience as emperor. He recalls his youthful enthusiasm for the republic and his intention of bringing the state back to self-government. He had thought Augustus hypocritical, because the latter claimed the same goal, yet could never resign his power. Now Claudius is in the same spot. He realizes that no one really wants the republic back, and the only people who wish to depose him are persons who want to be emperor in his place. Moreover, he used to be appalled at the crimes of Augustus's wife Livia, yet now he realizes that his own wife had been as ruthless and self-seeking with much less wisdom than the old empress.

In spite of his foolish blindness to his wife's villainies, however, Claudius concludes that the general benevolence of his reign has reconciled his subjects to monarchy again. Thus, insofar as he has succeeded in ruling wisely, he has ironically undermined his own goal of restoring the republic. The people must hate tyranny to overthrow it.

Using this curious reverse logic, Claudius makes a remarkable decision not to restrain the evil that might at last teach Rome the folly of obedience to despots. "Rome is fated to bow to another Caesar. Let him be mad, bloody, capricious, wasteful, lustful."

This resolve presumably provides the motivation for Claudius's seemingly foolish marriage to yet another unscrupulous, ambitious woman, his own niece Agrippina, daughter of Germanicus and Agrippina the elder. He also obligingly adopts her son Nero, who promises to fit the grisly requirements listed above for his successor.

Claudius thinks he has a scenario for the future all worked out. His own son Britannicus he keeps carefully isolated from the degenerating influence of court life and plans to hide him far away with a friendly queen in Britain. Then after the disaster almost certain to befall Rome in the reign of Nero, his own son can come back as a popular hero to help reconstruct the republic. This somewhat fanciful dream is rudely shattered, however, when Britannicus declines his role, insisting that he can deal with his stepbrother right there at home. (History has proved his confidence unwarranted, since Nero, shortly after he became emperor, had Britannicus assassinated.) Thus, the evil that

Claudius foresees certainly comes to pass, but not the
hoped-for redemption.

Claudius ends his days as a pawn of his wife and his
freedmen. The novel closes with an addendum to the autobiographical narrative: three accounts of his death, according to the ancient chroniclers Suetonius, Tacitus, and Dio
Cassius. All agree that he was poisoned by his wife.

Few historical novels are so faithful to reality, so far as
it can be known, as these two books. There are no purely
fictional characters, and practially all the events have an
historical source (though the sources, of course, may be in
error). Ancient historians, particularly Suetonius, did not
always discriminate carefully between established fact and
court gossip.

Graves has imaginatively interpreted motivations for
historical action, of course, and elaborated some incidents
to suit his own purposes, especially where reports are ambiguous or contradictory. Many of the most fantastic episodes, however, such as the building of the bridge of ships,
or Caligula's throwing Claudius off a bridge into the river,
or the weird harassment of Germanicus before he died, are
quite accurate transcriptions of their sources, with only the
addition of the autobiographical point of view. As Mary
McCarthy said of *I, Claudius*, when it was first published:

In no respect is Mr. Graves guilty of writing history to suit his
fancy, though, if presented with two tenable theories, he will, like
any lively biographer, choose the more dramatic. His book is
amazingly full of color and imagination.[1]

Graves admits in the author's note that precedes
Claudius the God that Claudius's defeat of the British chieftain Caractacus posed special difficulty because of the mea-
gerness of contemporary reports. The details of the campaign, therefore, may be more a creation by Graves than by
Claudius. It is certainly plausible, however, that Claudius's
style as a warrior should come closer to Odysseus, who
conceived the Trojan horse, than to Achilles, who killed the

mighty Hector. With the aid of considerable scholarly knowledge, Claudius wins the battle for Britain by clever ruses, good strategy, and unusual weapons.

Depending upon the attitude of the reviewer, faithfulness to historical sources may win either praise or blame. Graves himself has apparently resented the fact that "some reviewers" said he had simply put together and expanded a little the accounts of Tacitus and Suetonius. In the author's note preceding *Claudius the God*, where he makes this complaint, he lists a great many other sources:

Among Classical writers who have been borrowed from in the composition of *Claudius the God* are Tacitus, Dio Cassius, Suetonius, Pliny, Varro, Valerius Maximus, Crosius, Frontinus, Strabo, Caesar, Columell, Plutarch, Josephus, Diodorus Siculus, Photius, Xiphilinus, Zonaras, Seneca, Petronius, Juvenal, Philo, Colsus, the authors of the *Acts of the Apostles* and of the pseudogospels of Nicodemus and St. James, and Claudius himself in his surviving letters and speeches.

There are certain ironic implications in both the charge of simply expanding the best known sources and Graves's defense of depending upon a broad background of research. Presumably, to use only two sources is excessively derivative, but to use many is scholarly. But the issue of authenticity to history is one of the hazards of writing historical fiction. The writer risks censure from experts if he distorts historical records, or, again, if he leans on them too heavily. The ordinary reader may depend upon Graves, in this case, I believe, to offer an accurate impression of first century Rome, either as it really was or as it was thought to be by early chroniclers.

But the real challenge of writing historical fiction is not just the problem of historical accuracy. It is the more subtle one of combining factual truth with literary purposes. Writers of historical romance sometimes deal with this problem by creating fictional characters with fictional conflicts that may be plausibly inserted into historical contexts.

Thus, historicity is simply an added attraction, part of the window-dressing for conventional plots. But obviously Graves has not done this.

He deals with the stuff of history itself. But he orders and elaborates fact to reveal some of the complex relationships between human character and historical events, which presumably have continuous relevance to human life.

The role of history is to recount what once happened. The role of literature is more nearly that ascribed to poetry by Aristotle: it reveals the universal qualities in particular experience. Aristotle said that these general truths about human nature are more important than the particular truths of history.

Thus, historical fiction, even when it sticks so closely to recorded events as Graves does in these novels, is necessarily some kind of hybrid. It uses historical events to reveal the ways human beings may act in different social and political situations. To quote Avrom Fleishman's perceptive definition of the grand theme of historical fiction: "the relation of personal loyalties, values, and passions to the network of historical forces which surround and condition them."[2]

What, then, are these universal truths that the writer perceives in the particulars of history?

The Claudius novels are studies in the dynamics of power: how power is acquired, how it corrupts most persons who seek it, how it victimizes so many others. Under the sober account of a rather timid participant runs a tragic sense of life, wherein the good usually die young. Only fools can beat the odds. And when a wise fool like Claudius attains power, corruption does not cease, despite his good intentions. Claudius, who became emperor when he was fifty years old, thought he could change his world and perhaps reestablish the republic. His final wisdom, however, is closer to that of Sysiphus, who, in Greek mythology, was doomed forever to push a boulder up the mountain, only to see it roll down again, his hard labors wasted.

It would be easy to oversimplify what the novels suggest about the effects of power, however. One could repeat the well-known statement attributed to Lord Acton, "Power corrupts, absolute power corrupts absolutely." While this is a widely applicable observation, it does not account precisely for the gradations of evil displayed by the Caesars and their associates.

Caligula remains the prime example of the overwhelming potential for evil in absolutely unrestrained freedom of action. Yet, did power corrupt him? According to *I, Claudius*, he was a cruel patricide long before he became emperor. Power only enlarged his opportunities for evil and fed his dangerous delusions.

A few persons seem to withstand the temptations of power though they are inevitably changed in some ways. Augustus was not conspicuously corrupt, but no doubt was misled often enough by others, and sometimes unjust or even cruel. Germanicus had most of the requirements for being a powerful leader, for he was beloved by both the common people and the Roman army. He was a model of everything noble in a Roman soldier: brave, honest, and loyal. If he had also more distrust and self-seeking in his nature, he could easily have snatched the reins of government from Tiberius after Augustus died.

Women seem particularly vicious in the Roman ambience, yet this is, in some sense, attributable to the limitations such a society forces upon them. When dynamic women such as Livia have no recognized outlets for their talents, they are likely to develop compensatory qualities. Poison is traditionally a woman's weapon simply because few others are available to her. And seduction remains one of the surest methods of attaining power in a society where women can rule only through men.

Livia had significant power in the Roman government because of her curious influence with Augustus, who for most of his reign trusted her implicitly. She was once married to Claudius's grandfather, but induced her husband to divorce her by claiming that the child she was carrying was not his. Divorces were frequent among the Roman nobility. A husband could divorce a woman without public explanation, return her with her dowry to her father, and keep the children. By pretending the unborn Tiberius was not her husband's child, Livia got her freedom to marry the emperor and kept her child, too. In order to marry Livia meanwhile, Augustus divorced his wife on the very day that she bore him a child. That child, of course, remained with its father.

Good women are not totally lacking, though they are usually powerless. Octavia, Augustus's sister and Mark Antony's widow, though of no importance to the story, is nonetheless a rare model of what a Roman matron was supposed to be—chaste and devoted to raising Antony's children (even those born to Cleopatra).

The one steadfastly loyal woman in Claudius's personal life is Calpurnia, a professional prostitute whom he keeps all his life. She is not necessarily a steady concubine, for she is retired to managing Claudius's country estate when Claudius marries Messalina. Unlike his wives, Calpurnia never deceives Claudius and sometimes rescues him from imminent disaster. While Caligula is busy bankrupting the nation, Calpurnia shrewdly foresees that when the money runs out, no rich man will be safe. She starts asking Claudius for gifts of cash, instead of the gowns or other finery he offers to get for her. This money goes into a secret cache for the future.

Just as she prophesied, Caligula soon reinstates an old law that encourages a class of professional informers. Citizens can be executed or banished for treason or blasphemy on the flimsiest pretexts. The estates of condemned persons are confiscated by the state, while the informer who brought the charge shares in the take. Obviously, condemnation of wealthy citizens becomes very profitable. Luckily, by that time Claudius is quite poor—not counting, of course, Calpurnia's secret hoard.

Her loyalty does not imply, however, any moral superiority for the poor and humble as a class. Yet there may be a muted implication that a pernicious class system can sometimes shut off the only satisfactory solution to a difficult situation. For a prostitute to marry a king was socially unthinkable, yet Calpurnia, had she had that opportunity, might have saved Claudius from those blunders with unscrupulous wives.

The effect of power on Claudius himself remains the central mystery of *Claudius the God*. The moral sensitivity exhibited in the scholar-recluse of the first novel does, to some extent, leach away. The clues are often casual, but quite explicit. When describing the grandeur of his triumph, for instance, he notes that he rode in a magnificent, gold-plated chariot very like the one that he had condemned as being ostentatious in his more austere days. When he first attends a gladiatorial contest as a youth, he mortifies his family by fainting when a contestant is bloodily killed. He recalls this incident much later as he obviously relishes a staged sea battle he had devised for entertainment wherein many are killed. He acquires, in other words, the tastes and perhaps the vices of his class.

His emotional vulnerability to beautiful women may be only tangentially a result of power. Such women probably sooth the bruised ego of a man who has been openly despised and forced in his youth to marry a monstrous and dangerous woman. As in his invasion of Britain, imperial power gave him at least the semblance of equality with other men of his class. This is an understandable weakness that might plague any man so handicapped.

Though not inevitably corrupting, therefore, power so exaggerates the consequences of human frailty that normal error can assume tragic proportions.

Since these novels are written as Claudius's autobiography, they lack the unity that more purely fictional creations demonstrate. The reality of an entire life is never so neatly ordered and logical as a tightly constructed plot.

Certainly this pseudo-autobiography is remarkable

more for its richness of detail than for its unity. We become enmeshed in the precarious lives of persons dominated by powerful personalities. There are, as well, fascinating stories within the story, such as the career of Claudius's friend, Herod Agrippa, who, as an eastern king, thought himself to be the promised Jewish messiah. To anyone fascinated with the results of Graves's historical research, the episodic nature of the account is not a burden.

I, Claudius is structurally a more satisfactory novel than *Claudius the God,* however. This is primarily due to the clarity of the conflict in the first novel.

The two threads of meaning that, intertwined, give some unity to *I, Claudius* are these: the ruthlessness of Augustus's wife, Livia, who plots to retain and enlarge her powers beyond her husband's death; and the vulnerability of Claudius, who watches helplessly from the sidelines as one after another of his friends and relatives are destroyed. Moreover, the book achieves a heightened suspense when Livia, the initial adversary, dies. Livia was a prudent and competent executive, but Caligula, who takes over her function as adversary, is lacking all restraint. The combination of cruelty and insanity makes Claudius's position more dangerous than ever. Thus, the novel works up to a natural climax at the end, when Claudius expects to be swept away with his hated nephew.

By contrast with this rising vector of interest, *Claudius the God* seems to be a relatively level tour of the plateau of Claudius's power. His problems are political and strategic ones, seldom seen as personally dangerous to the protagonist. Not until the plot involving Messalina is there any real consciousness of possible disaster. And the integrity of the natural climax of the novel rests with the plausibility of Claudius's reaction to that event. Thus, Graves is not depending upon historical events so much, at this point, as upon an imagined psychic event. That event, the painful self-examination that leads to a deliberately destructive marriage, has only marginal plausibility.

Plausibility, of course, is extremely important in fiction. Historians show Claudius to be simply flabby in judgment, at this point, and unduly influenced by the people around him. But that would not matter, if Graves could create a plausible illusion of mental strength and rational decision.

Graves has accurately dramatized, in the crisis with Messalina, however, what Tacitus called "Claudius' sluggish uxoriousness."[3] Actually, in both the novel and in historical accounts, a subordinate arranged Messalina's death before she came to trial, because Claudius's associates were afraid he would be soft as putty if Messalina ever actually appeared before him. To follow this convincing show of real weakness with a remarkable mental and emotional transformation in which weakness is deliberately feigned—or at least indulged with an understanding of the consequences—involves considerable risk.

But there may be a technical reason for this literary device. Graves apparently wished to preserve the character of Claudius as tragic, not simply pathetic. Therefore, Claudius must not decline, as he probably did in real life, into a rather foolish old age. He must retain the dignity of free choice in his own downfall.

The mythos of tragedy requires that a protagonist be at least partially responsible for his own destruction. The tragic hero recognizes evil in the world and makes a commitment to fight that evil. But he commits some grievous error in the process and brings about his own disaster. That error must be willfully chosen, not just stumbled into. If this is the scenario Graves had in mind, he was faced with a rather intractable reality that does not fit easily into the mold.

Yet, the psychological conflict of a man with his own nature is often a more profound theme than a conflict with some external force. The stoic Epictetus once said that the common man sees evil outside himself, but the wise man knows that it dwells within. Certainly, Claudius has his flaw of pride. Though effectively muffled by circumstances dur-

ing his first fifty years, it emerges modestly with his ascent to
the throne. Perhaps if the fictional Claudius had indicated
any conflict between aspiration and performance during his
more vigorous years of power, one might more easily accept
his late claim to idealism about reestablishing the republic.

If Graves did not intend to preserve Claudius as a tragic
figure, then Claudius's apparent achievement of self-
knowledge is a lesser vehicle—simply an old man's futile
hindsight. Again, one must sympathize with the difficulty
of Graves's task in retaining sympathy and admiration for a
character who simply unravels at the end.

15

The Myth behind
the Myths of Graves

The career of Robert Graves almost defies analysis—a fact that no doubt pleases him well. He has always resisted the "eyes that fix you in a formulated phrase,"[1] and the academic impulse that pins the neatly classified specimen on the wall. This butterfly has made an art of flying crooked, and to observe him impaled upon a pin is necessarily misleading.[2]

Perhaps the only suitable approach to so eccentric a personality is one developed for the interpretation of myth by one of the most recent innovators in that field. According to the structural analysis of Claude Lévi-Strauss, the elements of myth are factors that mediate contradictories in a dialectic fashion. One must work with all known variations of a related set of myths. Thus Lévi-Strauss tabulates South American Indian myths that involve complicated relationships between polar opposites: origin of fire and origin of antifire (wind and rain), incestuous kinship relations and murderous kinship relations, raw food (perceived as natural) and cooked food (perceived as cultural). The process seems to call for an exquisitely programmed computer, which would provide algebraic formulae corresponding to the web of meaning peculiar to a particular society.

Obviously such a process was not designed to analyze the web of meaning peculiar to a particular person. Yet, if structural analysis shows there is a logic (non-Aristotelian, I presume) beyond seemingly nonrational, capricious, even outright contradictory ideas and emotions, then perhaps someday some combined literary critic-mythologist-psycho-historian with a computer will explain Robert Graves. The logic of the primitive set of myths operates unconsciously, however. How many dimensions must be added for the pos-sibility of consciously assumed pose—the suspicion that Graves is often only half-serious, laughing into his sleeve?

Even so, Graves's career seems to be an oscillation between contradictory positions, which may (like Lévi-Strauss's sets of contrapuntal myths) make sense in a cul-tural context. How ironic it would be if future "social scien-tists" would regard Graves as their favorite case history, dramatizing a basic conflict between rationalistic, techno-logical, modern society and an older poetic, religious, ro-mantic sensibility! Nor will Graves emerge wholly in the second of these camps, but rather wandering in some un-certain no-man's-land between. He is, after all, a coolly calculating exploder of myths as well as a promoter of his own favorite monomyth.

In his personal dialectic of belief he has begun in a thoroughly conventional, fundamentalist Christianity, swung to an equally conventional liberal, socialistic athe-ism, to arrive ultimately at a nonpolitical, aesthetic doc-trine (only quasireligious) as expressed in the mythology of the white goddess. This archaic set of symbols has not only fed his poetic creativity, but also seems to mirror his own stormy relationships with strong-minded women.

This personal application is no doubt beyond the scope of a mere reader untrained in psychoanalysis. Yet, the ad-mitted autobiographical elements in such troubled works as "The Shout" and "But It Still Goes On," the weird, un-healthy glow of *No Decency Left* and *The Antigua Stamp*, the dreamlike *Watch the North Wind Rise*, the cool revela-tions of *Goodbye to All That*, all invite personal observa-tions about the man as well as his work.

Moreover, Graves launched his serious career in poetry under the influence of the Freudian psychologist, Rivers. Graves was convinced then, at least, of the relevance of dreams to poetic creativity and the psychologically therapeutic function of poetry in working out emotional conflicts. Not only did he later reject his former psychological views, he vehemently repudiated all psychological explanations of myth. Yet, the strength of his denial of Freudian and Jungian contributions to myth theory appears to be directly correlated to their relevance to himself.

Randall Jarrell has been most outspoken about the precision with which Graves lived and relived the White Goddess myth, particularly in his relationship to Laura Riding, before he ever made it a written article of poetic faith. Says Jarrell, "She [Riding] seems to have had a radical influence on Graves' life, poetry, and opinions until 1939; and it was only after Graves was no longer in a position to be dominated by her in specific practice that he worked out his general theory of the necessary dominance of the White Goddess, the Mother-Muse, over all men, all poets."[3] Jarrell writes with a somewhat unnecessary condescension of the psychological implications of the White Goddess, yet his point seems hard to refute:

One does not need much of a psychoanalytic or anthropological background to see that Graves' world-picture is a projection upon the universe of his own unconscious, of the compulsively repeated situation in which, alone, it is able to find satisfaction; or to see that this world-picture is one familiar, in structure and in much detail in the fantasies of children and neurotics, in dreams, in fairy-tales, and, of course, in the myths and symbols of savages and of earlier cultures.[4]

Jarrell refers his readers to an essay by Jung on "The Relations Between the Ego and the Unconscious."

So stung was Graves by this psychological dismissal of his aesthetic-mythological orientation, that he defiantly quoted Jarrell in a public address. Then he neatly turned the argument away by suggesting that Freud and Jung were the ones who projected their private fantasies upon the universe. He got his by scholarly research into ancient religions. I suspect that both Jarrell's and Graves's views of the issue are, in some sense "true," though not the whole truth, just as those seemingly contradictory South American myths combine to mean something that transcends the opposites. Though in Aristotelian logic P and *not-P* are mutually exclusive, in metaphorical thinking other rules may prevail. Graves actually has an impressive store of knowledge about the past. Moreover, he is honest about the fusion of his own intuition with the available evidence. But what he brings forth from the grave is his own image.

That, in itself, does not necessarily invalidate his worldview either of the present or of the past. After all, one of the tenets of his personal philosophy is that the true poet is essentially the same in function and motivation, whether he lived then or now or in the future. Ideally he acts as oracle and prophet, speaking the truths of the human spirit and interpreting the demands of a personified nature upon it.

To pursue further my speculative analogy between Graves's literary production and a set of myths, here is Edmund Leach, writing on the nature of myth in *Genesis as Myth*, an application of structural analysis:

Myths proper lack a chronology in any strict sense, for the beginning and the end must be apprehended simultaneously; significance is to be discerned only in the relations between the component parts of the story; sequence is simply a persistent rearrangement of elements which are present from the start.[4]

Graves would agree with this observation, perhaps, since he sang of the "one story only," which repeats itself endlessly in a round of birth, love, and death, in the sometimes nurturing, sometimes threatening shadow of the Eternal Female. Yet the passage is relevant to Graves's literary themes, whether prose or poetry, and to his personal experience as well. In spite of his seemingly radical shifts of orientation, there is that "persistent rearrangement of elements which are present from the start"—or at least from World War I and the shattering of his naive, conventional view of life.

The ambivalent character of the White Goddess haunted his poetry and prose long before he realized her place in history. And the personal, psychological element in his vision of the Goddess persisted even as he protested "She is not *my* White Goddess," pointing to the long ago and far away.

This is not to suggest that the White Goddess is "merely" a projection of Graves's imagination. Modern archeological scholarship supports his claims for the widespread goddess cults of Neolithic times. And the evidence for the preeminence of women in the social-religious life of that time, while not conclusive, is certainly impressive.

These observations about women are timely and provide a needed corrective to the exclusively masculine bias of western history. If nothing else, Graves's somewhat eccentric impulse to rewrite history reminds us that what is perpetuated as historical fact is often quite arbitrary. Graves may be at least partly responsible, along with other factors such as the emergence from obscurity of minority races, for a new sophistication about what has been accepted unquestioningly about the past. Historians, historical novelists, mythologists, anthropologists are all engaged in an imaginative reconstruction of the past, with personal bias inevitably coloring interpretation.

What is even more fascinating is that an ancient set of religious symbols still resonates in a modern mind, directing the imagination of one of our more impressive users of language. His absorbtion of these archaic thought patterns must indicate that they are emotionally and intellectually viable in some as yet unexplained way. Edmund Leach, in the work quoted above, suggests that some underlying mental structures are common to all members of a society and possibly to the whole species. He implies that both poetry and myth tap this associational level of meaning.

Whenever a corpus of mythology is recited in its religious setting such structural patterns are 'felt' to be present, and convey meaning much as poetry conveys meaning. Even though the ordinary listener is not fully conscious of what has been communicated, the 'message' is there in a quite objective sense.... Furthermore it seems evident that much the same patterns exist in the most diverse kinds of mythology. This seems to be a fact of great psychological, sociological and scientific significance. Here truly are observable phenomena which are the expression of unobservable realities.[5]

Whether structural analysis can make some striking revelations about how and why people (including Graves) think the way they do remains to be seen. It is a tantalizing possibility. Myth interpretation also advances through a dialectic of apposing methodologies. The conspicuous example is the long feud between two brilliant adversaries— Max Müller with his solar mythology and Andrew Lang with his anthropological, approach. Meanwhile, a ritualist like Lord Raglan, believing that all myth derives from religious rite, spent much of his energy attacking the euhemerists, who proposed that myths, like the legends that develop around an Abraham Lincoln or Davy Crockett, derived originally from historical persons or events.

Actually, some of the criticism leveled at Graves for his views on myth comes from ardent supporters of this or that narrowly restricted view. Some interpret his eclecticism as simply flabby scholarship, a complaint that may in some cases be justified. In *The Greek Myths*, Graves does combine, or at least place side by side, issues classifiable as ritualistic, semantic, iconotropic, anthropological, euhemerist. The purist steeped in a particular methodology cannot abide such miscellaneous possibilities.

This difficulty does not disturb the general reader and may, I suspect, enhance the value of Graves's books for the nonexpert.[6] My admittedly inexpert complaint about Graves as a mythologist is that he rigorously excluded, as I have noted above, the psychological implications of myth, which also deserve a hearing. I cannot believe that anyone is in possession of the final truth on this subject. I applaud the eminent good sense of Stith Thompson, who delivered the final address in an impressive symposium on myth, which included most of the recognized mythologies and theories.

There have doubtless been actual sun-myths and star-myths and moon-myths, and I am persuaded by reading in Laister and in von der Leyen's book on the folktale that some myths and tales may have come from dreams—always, of course, in terms of life as known by the dreamer. . . . I know that certain of my friends, well acquainted at firsthand with the stories of certain primitive peoples, are persuaded that occasionally psychoanalytical interpretations of some variety do actually apply. And my objection to the ritualistic school is not based upon a disbelief in the possibility of ritual producing myth or to doubt as to its actual occurrence in the Mediterranean area and sometimes in unlettered tribes of Australia and North America. It is to the exclusive claims of all these schools that objection is to be raised.[7]

Graves does, it is true, push his interpretation (ritualistic, euhemerist, whatever) to support his unified, not scientifically provable view of the development of patriarchal society from matriarchal beginnings. This automatically weights the evidence somewhat. Yet, he is easily deflected into other avenues of thought. As I have noted elsewhere, much of *The Hebrew Myths*, perhaps because of the leavening influence of his collaborator, Patai, is traditional Hebrew (that is to say, patriarchal) interpretation.

Much of the animosity directed toward Graves is not really attributable to his scholarship, good or bad, however, but to his value judgments. Unlike the nineteenth century Bachofen, who claimed that civilization *advanced* from matriarchy to patriarchy, Graves presents the change as unmitigated disaster, from which spring all the evils of capitalism, technology, and war. He has also had the temerity to apply comparative methods to Christian mythology, still widely tabooed for some kinds of intellectual inquiry. Thus, for some hypersensitives, he is a trespasser on private intellectual domains, a traitor to his own sex, and a pernicious misleader of youth.

Though his elevation of the Female to godhead is con-

venient in feminist terms and entertaining for those simply
annoyed with orthodox, unthinking sexism, it is nevertheless a mixed blessing. It attacks some stereotypes (for which
women may be grateful) but reinforces others. It says far
more, I suspect, about a male mythopoeic view of women
than it does about female nature. Is it really flattering that
the man can be in love with a woman only if she conforms
to an archetype already dear to his heart?

Though he has written many good love lyrics, the beloved woman never emerges with any individual characteristics. Nor can he achieve, at least in poetry, the gentle
mockery of his own literary convention, such as Shakespeare did when he wrote: "My mistress' eyes are nothing like
the sun,/Coral is far more red than her lips' red,/ If snow be
white, why then her breasts are dun,/ If hairs be wires, black
wires grow on her head." *Watch the North Wind Rise* is, to
be sure, a light-hearted, ironic treatment of his own
myth—and charming for that very reason.

His historical novels, though remarkably diverse in
plot and setting, also exhibit stylized women. Some of them
are fascinating creatures, but they usually conform to the
White Goddess character and temperament, even before
Graves had written her gospel. Livia, in *I, Claudius*, displays all the power, worldly wisdom, and ruthlessness of the
Triple Goddess as Crone. Messalina and Agrippina are si-
rens and witches on a smaller scale. They generally prevail
over Claudius, as Livia controls the god-emperor Augustus.

Antonina and the Empress Theodora in *Count Belisarius*, for all their token Christianity, are thoroughly pagan. They are indomitable in protecting those they love,
ruthless in avenging slights, eminently intelligent and sensible even when men are foolish or pretentious. In *The
Islands of Unwisdom*, Doña Isabel, though seductive, has
not an ounce of gentleness about her. She destroys men
who oppose her and cancels out the ineffectual altruism of
both her husband and her lover. Even Kate Harlowe is
more at home in the American wilderness than stuffy

Sergeant Lamb will ever be. She knows no sense of duty except to her own nature. Mary the Hairdresser of *King Jesus*, of course, is the embodiment of the Goddess on earth, the Crone who is both Queen of the Harlots and the Layer-Out who officiates at the death of the Sacred King.

The young virgin Nausicaa of *Homer's Daughter* is perhaps the most benevolent of the heroines, though the wholesale slaughter of her suitors belies that description. Mary Powell Milton is the most feeble—the goddess ignominiously dethroned by the male usurper. The Puritans destroy her queendom, the half-pagan countryside of Merry England with its rich tradition of festivals in celebration of nature.

Where honor, duty, patriotism, or Christian morality may motivate men, they have little relevance to women, who seem to represent the more elemental cycles of nature. These are ultimately triumphant over the sometimes civilizing, but largely futile, efforts of mankind to mold nature to their own desires. As one of Graves's poems points out, "Man Does, Woman Is." Jesus, who makes war upon the Female, nevertheless replays the ancient role of the sacrificed Sacred King.

Though men are the doers, their achievements are seldom permanent. How much did the exploits of a Belisarius or a Sergeant Lamb or a Don Alvaro or a Claudius change the structure or destiny of their world? It was as though they had never been. Belisarius, for all his brilliance, could not preserve the Byzantine Empire for long, nor could Claudius reactivate the Roman Republic. Sergeant Lamb fought on the losing side of the American Revolution, and the Solomon Islands were lost to Europeans for almost two hundred years after Don Alvaro's abortive attempt at colonization.

Human greed and folly, balanced by the persistent human need for love and propagation, bring so-called advancements back to nature's norm. There is an unfailing fountainhead of energy in the nonrational—and women know this better than men. That is why, at least in Graves's stereotyped view of gender differences, Fate is appropriately female and, like Mother Night, the Goddess behind all gods.

One might object that the strange case of Jesus, called the Christ, has reversed the trend. In spite of his reenactment of the ancient ritual of the Sacred King, who is the Goddess's consort, he established once and for all the dominance of the male principle. Yet the novels about the post-Christian world suggest that Christianity has made but little impact on human character and destiny. Milton brought paradise no closer, for all his immortalizing the Garden as God's domain, where the Mother of All Living, its former owner, had no right to pick the apples.

Notes

1. Biography

1. All subsequent personal statements by Graves are taken from there, unless otherwise noted.
2. T. S. Matthews, *Jacks or Better* (New York: Harper & Row, 1977), p. 331.
3. Briffault and Bachofen posited an early matriarchal stage in social development. See especially Bachofen's *Das Mutter-recht*, first published in Germany in 1861, currently available as *Myth, Religion & Mother Right* (Princeton, N.J.: Princeton University Press, 1973). Jane Harrison wrote on the backgrounds of Greek religion, especially the role of the goddess Themis, representing natural order. Margaret Murray investigated witchcraft cults, considering them as remnants of the "old religion," rather than Christian heresies. See John B. Vickery, *Robert Graves and the White Goddess* (Lincoln: University of Nebraska Press, 1972) for a discussion sion of Graves's indebtedness to James Frazer's *The Golden Bough*.

2. The White Goddess and the Art of Poetry

1. Daniel Hoffman, *Barbarous Knowledge* (New York: Oxford University Press, 1967), p. 157.
2. J. M. Cohen, *Robert Graves* (New York: Oxford University Press, 1967), p. 157.
3. E. O. James, *The Cult of the Mother Goddess* (New York: Frederick A. Praeger, 1959).

4. Erich Neumann, *The Great Mother* (Princeton, N.J., Princeton University Press, 1955).

3. THE WHITE GODDESS AND *The Greek Myths*

1. *Epilegoma & Themis* (New York: University Books, 1962), p. 485. *Themis* was first published in 1912.
2. For a discussion of Graves's probable sources for the White Goddess mythology see John B. Vickery *Robert Graves and the White Goddess* (Lincoln: University of Nebraska Press, 1972).
3. Herbert Weisinger, *The Agony and the Triumph* (East Lansing: Michigan State University Press, 1961).
4. Ibid., p. 140.
5. Joseph Campbell, *The Masks of God: Occidental Mythology* (New York: The Viking Press, 1964), p. 7.
6. In the myth, the winged horse Pegasus sprang from the dead body of Medusa, after Perseus had beheaded her.
7. Jane E. Harrison, *Prolegomena to the Study of Greek Religion* (1922: reprint ed., New York: Arno Press, 1976), p. xxxiii.
8. E. O. James, *The Cult of the Mother Goddess* (New York: Frederick A. Praeger, 1959), p. 228.
9. Ibid., p. 11.
10. Jay Macpherson, "Review Article: *The Greek Myths*," *Phoenix* Vol. 12, No. 1 (Spring, 1958), p. 21.
11. Campbell, *The Masks of God*, p. 86.
12. G. S. Kirk, *The Nature of the Greek Myths* (Middlesex, England., 1974), p. 38.

4. POETRY

1. We have lingered in the chambers of the sea
   By sea-girls wreathed with seaweed red and brown
   Till human voices wake us, and we drown.
   —T. S. ELIOT,
   "The Love Song of J. Alfred Prufrock."
2. See "The White Goddess" in *5 Pens in Hand*, p. 57.

3. J. M. Cohen, *Robert Graves* (New York: Grove Press, 1960),
    p. 108.
4. Douglas Day, *Swifter Than Reason* (Chapel Hill, University
    of North Carolina Press, 1963).
5. Ibid., pp. 35–36.
6. Quoted by Michael Kirkham in "Robert Graves's Debt to
    Laura Riding," *Focus on Robert Graves*, No. 3, Dec. 1973.
    Originally from *Epilogue* III (Majorca: Seizin Press, 1937).

5. Novels Using Greek Myth

1. Zeus swallowed the woman he made pregnant with Athene.
    Months later Zeus suffered from a terrible headache. The
    artisan god of the forge, Haephastus, then split Zeus's head
    open to relieve the pain. Out jumped Athene with a great
    shout, fully clothed in armor. She was known as a battle
    goddess, but was primarily in defense of the city and its
    civilized arts and crafts. She was also associated with wis-
    dom, since she combined female intuition with male intelli-
    gence. She was, so to speak, the mouthpiece of Zeus.
2. When Orpheus's bride died of snakebite, Orpheus went to
    the underworld to bring her back. His marvelous music
    charmed the three-headed dog, Cerberus, that guarded the
    entrance, as well as Hades and Persephone, the king and
    queen of the underworld. Although Orpheus returned to the
    upper world unharmed, he lost his wife because he turned to
    look at her before she had passed through the gates. Perse-
    phone had warned him not to look back until they were free
    of death's realm.

6. Graves and the Mythological Future

1. One must remember that in Graves the Goddess usually
    appears as the fatal "other woman," rather than as the lawful
    wife.
2. Martin Seymour-Smith, *Robert Graves* (London: Long-
    mans, Green & Co., 1956), p. 11.

7. HEBREW MYTHOLOGY

1. Joseph Gaer, *The Lore of the Old Testament* (Boston: Little, Brown and Company, 1951).

2. Louis Ginsburg, *The Legends of the Jews,* Vol. I (Philadelphia: The Jewish Publication Society of America, 1911), p. xi. This volume covers the same expanse as the Graves-Patai book.

3. Moses Hadas, *Reporter* 30:45 (April 9, 1964).

4. Even in modern times, the very existence of the Israeli nation in Africa rests upon that ancient sacred charter about the Promised Land.

5. Graves, "Mushroom and Religion," in *Difficult Questions Easy Answers* (Garden City, N.Y.: Doubleday, 1973), p. 94.

6. Theodore H. Gastor, in *Saturday Review* 47:44 (March 21, 1964).

7. Cyrus H. Gordon, "Canaanite Mythology" in *Mythologies of the Ancient World,* ed. Samuel Noah Kramer (Garden City, N.Y.: Doubleday, 1961), p. 195.

8. Fitz Roy Richard Somerset Raglan, *The Hero* (London: Methuen and Co., Ltd., 1936).

9. Gastor, *Saturday Review.*

10. Frank Kermode, *Encounter* 23:69 (December 1964).

11. Gehazi's seduction has no biblical basis, though at a later date he succumbed to another kind of temptation. He accepted costly gifts from a man whom Elisha cured of leprosy. As a result, Gehazi was himself stricken with leprosy.

12. Biblically, of course, Elisha lived long after this episode. He was still around when the Shunamite and her son came back from seven years among the Philistines.

13. *Spectator* 135:340 (August 29, 1925).

8. SEARCH FOR THE HISTORICAL JESUS:
The Nazarene Gospel Restored

1. Graves, "Jewish Jesus... Gentile Christ," *New Republic* 135: 25–27.

2. Raphael Patai, *Hebrew Installation Rites* (Cincinnati: 1947).

3. Moses Hadas, *The New York Times* (July 18, 1954).

4. H. J. McLachilian, *Hibbert Journal* 53:315 (April, 1954).

9. *King Jesus*

1. Mark II, 13: "And seeing a fig tree afar off having leaves, he came, if haply he might find any thing thereon: and when he came to it, he found nothing but leaves; for the time of figs was not yet. 14: And Jesus answered and said unto it, No man eat fruit of thee hereafter for ever. . . . 20: And in the morning, as they passed by, they saw the fig tree dried up from the roots."

2. James Frazer, *The Golden Bough*, 12 vols. (London: Macmillan & Co., 1915), vol. 9: pp. 355, 362–65, 412–23.

3. John B. Vickery, *Robert Graves and the White Goddess* (Lincoln: University of Nebraska Press, 1972), pp. 50–51.

4. In Matthew XIX, 12, Jesus says that his disciples should make themselves eunuchs for the sake of the Kingdom of Heaven.

5. Clement of Alexandria, *Stromata*, iii.

10.   SATIRICAL WRITINGS

1. Jonathan Swift suggested that the Irish poor sell their numerous children to English gentry for food, thus benefiting both their parents and the English landlords.

2. George Stade, *Robert Graves* (New York: Columbia University Press, 1967), pp. 26–27.

3. Edwin Muir, *Transition* (London and New York, 1926), pp. 188–89. Quoted by Daniel Hoffman, *Barbarous Knowledge* (Oxford University Press, 1967), p. 182.

4. An anonymous reviewer in the *Times Literary Supplement* (London: June 2, 1952) complained that by changing the style from extravagant to plain, Graves utterly misrepresents Apuleius, making an Oscar Wilde read like a Defoe.

5. Richmond Lattimore, tr., *The Iliad of Homer* (University of Chicago Press, 1951), p. 27.

11.   OTHER PROSE

1. Hart's book was published in England as *T. E. Lawrence: in Arabia and After*, and in America as *Colonel Lawrence, the Man Behind the Legend*.

12.   HISTORICAL NOVELS: ON MURDER, MILTON, AND THE SPANISH MAIN

1.   T. S. Matthews says in *Jacks or Better* that Graves may have equated Milton with the American poet Schuyler Jackson, who had recently displaced Graves in the affections of Laura Riding. If so, this, added to Graves's disapproval of Milton's poetic methods, might account for the peculiar bitterness of Graves's treatment of Milton. See T. S. Matthews, *Jacks or Better* (New York: Harper & Row, 1977), p. 239–40.

14.   HISTORICAL NOVELS: ON CLAUDIUS

1.   Mary McCarthy, *The Nation* 138:679 (June 13, 1934).
2.   Avrom Fleishman, *The English Historical Novel* (Baltimore, Md.: Johns Hopkins Press, 1971), p. 233.
3.   Michael Grant, tr., *Tacitus on Imperial Rome* (Baltimore, Md.: Penguin Books, 1956), p. 239.

15.   THE MYTH BEHIND THE MYTHS OF GRAVES

1.   T. S. Eliot, "The Love Song of J. Alfred Prufrock."
2.   Graves has a little poem called "Flying Crooked":

> The butterfly, a cabbage-white,
> (His honest idiocy of flight)
> Will never now, it is too late,
> Master the art of flying straight,
> Yet has—who knows so well as I?—
> A just sense of how not to fly:. . . .

3.   Randall Jarrell, "Graves and the White Goddess, Part II" *The Yale Review*, Vol. XLV, No. 2 (Dec., 1955), p. 473.
4.   Ibid., p. 474.
4.   Edmund Leach, *Genesis as Myth and Other Essays* (London: Jonathan Cape, 1969), p. 28. The title essay concerns the seemingly inconsistent messages about incest in the Old Testament. In some instances Jehovah punishes incest, in some rewards it. Leach says these stories mediate contradictory social attitudes: one, the taboo against incest, and two, the rule of endogamous marriage to keep the blood lines of

God's chosen people "pure." The taboo is broken in certain circumstances that receive a sacred sanction.

5.   Ibid., pp. 22–23.

6.   As I sometimes facetiously advise college students, if you want to know the real truth about something read *one* book by an expert. If you make the mistake of reading two experts on a controversial subject, you are again thrown into an agony of doubt. Thus, if you want to satisfy your curiosity about witchcraft, read Margaret Murray's *God of the Witches*, but do not touch Elliot Rose's *A Razor for a Goat*, which refutes Murray's theory.

7.   Stith Thompson, "Myths and Folktales," in Thomas A. Sedbeck, ed., *Myth: A Symposium* (Bloomington: Indiana University Press, 1958), p. 110.

Bibliography

Works by Robert Graves

Poetry

Over the Brazier. London: The Poetry Bookshop, 1916.
Goliath and David. London: Chiswick Press, 1916.
Fairies and Fusiliers. London: William Heinemann, 1917.
Treasure Box. London: Chiswick Press, 1919.
Country Sentiment. London: Martin Secker, 1920.
The Pier-glass. London: Martin Secker, 1921.
The Feather Bed. London: Hogarth Press, 1923.
Whipperginny. London: William Heinemann, 1923.
Mock Beggar Hall. London: Hogarth Press, 1924.
Robert Graves: The Augustan Books of Modern Poetry. London: Ernest Benn, 1925.
The Marmosite's Miscellany. London: Hogarth Press, 1925. (John Doyl, pseudonym)
Welshman's Hose. London: Fleuron, 1925.
Poems 1914–1926. London: William Heinemann, 1927; Garden City, N.Y.: Doubleday, 1929.
Poems 1914–1927. London: William Heinemann, 1927.
Poems 1929. London: Seizin Press, 1929.
Ten Poems More. Paris: Hours Press, 1930.
Poems 1926–1930. London: William Heinemann, 1931.
To Whom Else. Majorca: Seizin Press, 1931.
Poems 1930–1933. London: Arthur Barker, 1933.
Collected Poems. London: Cassell, 1938.
No More Ghosts. London: Faber and Faber, 1940.
Robert Graves—The Augustan Poets Series. Eyre & Spottiswoode, 1943.

Poems. London: Cassell & Co., 1945.

Collected Poems 1914–1947. London: Cassell, 1948.

Poems and Satires. London: Cassell, 1951.

Poems. London: Cassell, 1953.

Collected Poems. Garden City, N.Y.: Doubleday, 1955.

Poems Selected by Himself. Baltimore, Md.: Penguin Books, 1957.

The Poems of Robert Graves. Garden City, N.Y.: Doubleday, 1958.

Collected Poems. London: Cassell, 1959.

The Penny Fiddle. London: Cassell, 1960. (For children.)

Collected Poems. Garden City, N.Y.: Doubleday, 1961.

More Poems. London: Cassell, 1961.

The More Deserving Cases. Wiltshire, Eng.: Marlborough College Press, 1962.

New Poems. London: Cassell, 1962.

Ann at Highwood Hall. London: Cassell, 1964. (For children.)

Man Does, Woman Is. London: Cassell, 1964.

Love Respelt. London: Cassell, 1965.

Collected Poems. London: Cassell, 1965.

The Crane Bag. London: Cassell, 1969.

Advice from a Mother. London: Poem-of-the-Month Club, 1970.

Queen-Mother to New Queen. San Francisco: University of San Francisco: Lawton and Alfred Kennedy, 1970.

The Green-Sailed Vessel. London: Rota, 1971.

Poems: Abridged for Dolls and Princes. London: Cassell, 1971.

Poems, 1968–1970. London: Cassell, 1970; Garden City, N.Y.: Doubleday, 1971.

Poems, Selected by Himself. (4th revised) Baltimore, Md.: Penguin Books, 1972 (first revision 1957, 2nd 1961, 3rd 1966).

New Collected Poems. Garden City, N.Y.: Doubleday, 1977.

Critical and Miscellaneous Writings

On English Poetry. New York: Alfred A. Knopf, 1922.

The Meaning of Dreams. London: Cecil Palmer, 1924.

Contemporary Techniques of Poetry: A Political Analogy. London: Hogarth Press, 1925.

John Kemp's Wager. Oxford: Basil Blackwell, 1925.

Poetic Unreason and Other Studies. London: Cecil Palmer, 1925.

Impenetrability; or, The Proper Habit of English. London: Hogarth Press, 1926.

Another Future of Poetry. London: Hogarth Press, 1926.

Lars Porsena, or The Future of Swearing. New York: Kegan Paul, Trench, Trubner, 1927.

Lawrence and the Arabs. London: Jonathan Cape, 1927.

Lawrence and the Arabian Adventure. Garden City, N.Y., Doubleday, Doran & Co., 1928. (American edition of preceding entry.)

The English Ballad. London: Ernest Benn, 1927.

The Less Familiar Nursery Rhymes. London: Ernest Benn, 1927.

John Skelton (Laureate). London: Ernest Benn, 1927.

A Survey of Modernist Poetry. London: William Heinemann, 1927. (With Laura Riding.)

Mrs. Fisher or The Future of Humour. London: Kegan, Paul, Trench, Trubner, 1928.

A Pamphlet against Anthologies. London: Jonathan Cape, 1928. (With Laura Riding.)

The Real David Copperfield. London: Arthur Barker, 1933.

David Copperfield by Charles Dickens. New York: Harcourt, Brace and Co., 1934. (American edition of preceding entry.)

Old Soldiers Never Die by Private Frank Richards D. C. M., M.M. (Edited by Graves). London: Faber & Faber, 1933.

The Future of Swearing and Improper Language (revised). London: Kegan Paul, Trench, Trubner, 1936.

Old Soldier Sahib by Private Frank Richards (edited by Graves). London: Faber & Faber, 1936.

The Long Week-End, A Social History of Great Britain 1918–1939. London: Faber & Faber, 1940. (With Alan Hodge.)

Reader over Your Shoulder. London: Jonathan Cape, 1943. (With Alan Hodge.)

The White Goddess. London: Faber & Faber, 1948.

The Common Asphodel—Collected Essays on Poetry. London: Hamish Hamilton, 1949.

Occupation: Writer. New York: Creative Age Press, 1950.

The Nazarene Gospel Restored. London: Cassell, 1953. (With Joshua Podro.)

The Greek Myths. 2 vols. Baltimore, Md.: Penguin Books, 1955.

The Crowning Privilege. London: Cassell, 1955.

Adam's Rib. London: Trianon Press, 1955.

¡Catatrok! London: Cassell, 1956.

Jesus in Rome—A Historical Conjecture. London: Cassell, 1957. (With Joshua Podro.)

English and Scottish Ballads. London: William Heinemann, 1957.

5 Pens in Hand. Garden City, N.Y.: Doubleday, 1958.

Steps. London: Cassell, 1958.

Food for Centaurs. Garden City, N.Y.: Doubleday, 1960.

Greek Gods and Heroes. Garden City, N.Y.: Doubleday, 1960.

Myths of Ancient Greece. London: Cassell, 1961. (English edition of preceding entry.)

Selected Poetry and Prose. London: Hutchinson Educational, 1961.

The Big Green Book. New York: Crowell-Collier Press, 1962. (For children.)

Oxford Addresses on Poetry. London: Cassell, 1962.

The Siege and Fall of Troy. London: Cassell, 1962. (For children.)

Nine Hundred Iron Chariots. Cambridge: Massachusetts Institute of Technology Press, 1963.

Mammon. London: London School of Economics and Political Science, 1964.

The Hebrew Myths: The Book of Genesis. Garden City, N.Y.: Doubleday, 1964. (With Raphael Patai.)

El Fenomeno Del Turismo. Madrid: Bolaxos y ʾAquilar 1964. (Translated in *Majorca Observed.*)

Majorca Observed. London: Cassell, 1965.

Mammon and the Black Goddess. London: Cassell, 1965.

Difficult Questions Easy Answers. Garden City, N.Y.: Doubleday, 1973.

Autobiographical

Goodbye to All That. London: Jonathan Cape, 1929.

But It Still Goes On. London and Toronto: Jonathan Cape, 1930.

T. E. Lawrence to His Biographers. New York: Doubleday, Doran & Co., 1938.

Fiction

My Head! My Head! London: Martin Secker, 1925.

The Shout. London: Elkin Mathews & Marrot, 1929.

No Decency Left (pseud. Barbara Rich). London: Jonathan Cape, 1932. (With Laura Riding.)

I, Claudius. London: Arthur Barker, 1934.

Claudius the God. London: Arthur Barker, 1934.

'*Antigua, Penny, Puce.*' Majorca: Seizin Press, 1936.

The Antigua Stamp. New York: Random House, 1937. (American edition of preceding entry.)

Count Belisarius. London: Cassell, 1938.

Sergeant Lamb of the Ninth. London: Methuen & Co., 1940.

Sergeant Lamb's America. New York: Random House, 1940. (American edition of the preceding entry.)

Proceed, Sergeant Lamb. London: Methuen & Co., 1941.

The Story of Marie Powell, Wife to Mr. Milton. London: Cassell, 1943.

The Golden Fleece. London: Cassell, 1944.

Hercules, My Shipmate. New York: Creative Age Press, 1945. (American edition of preceding entry.)

King Jesus. New York: Creative Age Press, Inc., 1946.

Seven Days in New Crete. London: Cassell, 1949.

Watch the North Wind Rise. New York: Creative Age Press, 1949. (American edition of preceding entry.)

The Islands of Unwisdom. Garden City, N.Y.: Doubleday, 1949.

The Isles of Unwisdom. London: Cassell, 1950. (British edition of preceding entry.)

Homer's Daughter. London: Cassell, 1955.

They Hanged My Saintly Billy. London: Cassell, 1957.

Collected Short Stories. Garden City, N.Y.: Doubleday, 1964.

Translations

George Schwarz. *Almost Forgotten Germany.* Majorca: Seizin Press, 1936. (With Laura Riding.)

Lucius Apuleius. *The Transformation of Lucius.* Harmondsworth, Middlesex: Penguin Books, 1950.

Manuel de Jesus Galvan. *The Cross and the Sword.* Bloomington: Indiana University Press, 1955.

Pedro Antonio de Alarcon. *The Infant with the Globe.* London: Trianon Press, 1955.

George Sand. *Winter in Majorca* (with Jose Quadrado's Refutation of George Sand). London: Cassell, 1956.

Lucan Pharsalia. *Dramatic Episodes of the Civil Wars.* Baltimore, Md.: Penguin Books, 1956.

Gaius Suetonius Granquillus. *The Twelve Caesars.* Baltimore,
    Md.: Penguin Books, 1957.

Hesiod. *Fable of the Hawk and the Nightingale* (from *Works and
    Days*). Lexington, Kentucky: Stamperia del Santuccio M.
    Cm. Lix., 1959.

Homer's *Iliad—The Anger of Achilles.* Garden City, N.Y.:
    Doubleday, 1959.

The Comedies of Terence (edited by Graves). Garden City, N.Y.:
    Doubleday, 1962.

Oratio Creweiana MDCCCCLXII. New York: Oxford University
    Press, 1962.

Oratio Creweiana MDCCCCLXIV. New York: Oxford University
    Press, 1964.

The Rubaiyyat of Omar Khayaam. Baltimore, Md.: Penguin
    Books, 1972.

Books About Graves

Cohen, J. M. *Robert Graves.* New York: Grove Press, 1960.

Day, Douglas. *Swifter Than Reason.* Chapel Hill: The University
    of North Carolina Press, 1963.

Enright, D. J. *Robert Graves and the Decline of Modernism.* Sin-
    gapore: University of Malaya, n.d.[c. 1960].

Fraser, G. S. "The Postry of Robert Graves" in *Design and
    Rhetoric.* New York: Barnes & Noble, 1959.

Fussell, Paul. *The Great War and Modern Memory.* New York
    and London: Oxford University Press, 1975.

Hoffman, Daniel. *Barbarous Knowledge. Myth in the Poetry of
    Yeats, Graves, and Muir.* New York: Oxford University
    Press, 1967.

Kirkham, Michael. *The Poetry of Robert Graves.* New York: Ox-
    ford University Press, 1969.

Matthews, T. S. *Jacks or Better.* New York: Harper & Row, 1977.

Musgrove, Sydney. *The Ancestry of "The White Goddess."* Auck-
    land: University of Auckland, 1962. No. 62, English Series
    No. 4.

Seymour-Smith, Martin. *Robert Graves.* London: Longmans,
    Green & Co., 1956.

Stade, George. *Robert Graves.* New York: Columbia University
    Press, 1967.

BIBLIOGRAPHIES

Vickery, John B. *Robert Graves and the White Goddess*. Lincoln: University of Nebraska Press, 1972.

Higginson, Fred H. A *Bibliography of the Works of Robert Graves*. Hamden, Conn.: Archon Books, 1966.

Mason, Ellsworth. *Focus on Robert Graves*. No. 1, January 1972. Long Island, N.Y.: Hofstra University Library. (Graves's most recent publications, also location and information on Graves collections and scholars.)

Pownall, David E. "An Annotated Bibliography of Articles on Robert Graves" in *Focus on Robert Graves*. No. 2, December 1973. Ed. Ellsworth Mason, Boulder, Colo.: University of Colorado Library.

Index